make!

Cath Kidston

make!

Cath Kidston

make!

Cath Kidston

PHOTOGRAPHY BY PIA TRYDE

Quadrille
PUBLISHING

Contents

Introduction

Sewing and other crafts have had an amazing revival in the last few years. With so much mass-produced merchandise available now, people are turning away from the high street and towards traditional craft techniques to create unique pieces. We're tired of our clothes and our homes looking like everyone else's. And it's fantastic to see this movement spreading all across the country.

It's not cheap keeping up with changing fashions, but the projects in this book are made using the thrifty crafts of appliqué and embroidery – which require no expensive equipment or materials; in fact, most make use of old scraps of material you might already have. Each project is in itself a joy to make, and, once you have finished, you have the added pleasure of having created something precious and completely personal to you.

Each of the 48 projects in the following chapters uses one of the 16 design templates I have included in the back of the book. All your favourites are there – the cowboy, the sailing boat, an assortment of florals and, of course, Stanley my naughty terrier – plus a few more that I have created especially. Every project is fully explained with step-by-step instructions, along with handy hints and suggestions to help you on your way.

I have to admit that my own sewing skills are fairly basic, so the projects here are all easily achievable – with a little bit of patience! From the very simple to the more complicated, each project is based on the same techniques, which are outlined at the beginning of the book. Why not start off with a straightforward appliquéd T-shirt (page 88) or the egg cosies (page 34), before turning your hand to the more advanced cowboy skirt (page 82) or alphabet cushion (page 104). Each project has been given a skill level, rated from one to three, so you can easily identify which will suit your experience.

Ever since I was a little girl I have loved old printed fabrics, in fact the concept for my business was to take these wonderful vintage prints and place them in a practical modern setting. *Make!* is a continuation of this idea. What could be more satisfying than taking an original fabric design and using it to update an old skirt? And just because your bag will carry your groceries home from the shops, there's no reason why it can't be covered in flowers or brightly coloured spots!

These are, of course, just starting points. At the back of the book, I have included a few further ways you can use the templates, but the fun will be in adapting the designs yourself and creating your own ideas. I hope you have just as much fun with these projects as I have had putting together this book.

Cath Kidston

Techniques

This section sets out the basic techniques you will need to re-create all the items in the book – some are very simple, others a little more ambitious, so there should be something for all ages and skills! Check out our handy tool-kit suggestions as well, so that once you get started you'll have everything you need.

Workbox

WORKBOX AND FABRICS

One of the best things about appliqué and embroidery is that neither technique requires expensive or specialised equipment. If you don't already have a ragbag, crammed full of offcuts, remnants and fabric salvaged from outworn clothing, now's the time to start collecting!

SEWING WORKBOX

• **Needles** – A mixed packet contains medium-length 'sharps' for general sewing; shorter quilting needles for finer work; and crewel (embroidery) needles with long eyes. Triangular-pointed leather needles pierce hide without damage. Keep them safe in a felt-leaved book. (See page 122 to make your own.)

• **Thimble** – This may seem a little old-fashioned but it's a vital piece of kit. You need to protect your fingers if you are going to do a lot of sewing. Thimbles come in different sizes: choose one that fits snugly but not tightly on your forefinger.

• **Pins** – Choose longer ones with coloured heads that can be spotted easily on thicker fabrics. Store them in a pincushion.

• **Scissors** – You'll need two pairs: small embroidery scissors with narrow, pointed blades for cutting out intricate curves and clipping threads; and a general pair for larger appliqué shapes, paper and fabrics.

• **Sewing thread** – You will require several colours for each project, to match the fabrics that you use. You could buy lots of reels, but a good solution is to get a thread plait, which is woven from many different sewing cottons in ready-to-use lengths.

• **Marking tools** – You will need to draw in temporary guidelines for embroidery. Use a chalk pencil to show up on dark fabrics, like denim, and a dressmaker's fading-ink pen for lighter backgrounds. These helpful fibre-tips have a light-sensitive pigment, which disappears in a few days.

• **Pencil** – You'll also need an ordinary drawing pencil for tracing the outline templates onto Bondaweb when you are working iron-on appliqué.

BONDAWEB AND IRON-ON INTERFACING

Two innovative products that make traditional needlecrafts easier. Bondaweb consists of a fine layer of heat-sensitive glue attached to a paper backing. Use it to trace, cut out and fuse on appliqué shapes in one smooth process. (Always make sure that you iron Bondaweb to the reverse of patterned fabrics.) Lightweight non-woven iron-on Vilene interfacing is designed for dressmaking, but I've used it to transfer embroidery templates onto their background.

FABRICS

Like its sister patchwork, working appliqué is an ecological way of recycling old materials. The project instructions give the minimum amount needed if you are buying new fabric, but it's always useful to have some spare. Most of the projects use felt or cotton fabrics, but PVC, tweed, fleece and leather have their own distinctive qualities.

• **Felt** – Felt is easy to handle as it doesn't have a 'wrong' side and, because it's non-woven, it cannot fray. Try to get all-wool felt rather than children's craft felt, which is made from synthetic fibres. Felt does not launder well, so use it for accessories or garments that are dry-cleaned or cold hand-washed.

• **Cotton and Linen** – Wash and iron fabrics and garments before starting work. This will remove any dressing from new cloth; freshen up old materials; and ensure your finished projects will not shrink.

YOUR EMBROIDERED AND APPLIQUÉD PROJECTS REQUIRE SPECIAL AFTERCARE. WASH THEM GENTLY IN COLD WATER WITH A LIQUID HANDWASH OR SOAPFLAKES AND DRY FLAT. MORE ROBUST ARTICLES — TOWELS AND SHEETS — CAN BE MACHINE-WASHED ON A GENTLE CYCLE, BUT THEY SHOULD NOT BE TUMBLED DRY.

How to
Appliqué

All the appliqué projects in the book are created in the same way – by cutting out fabric shapes and fixing them onto a garment or accessory. If some of them appear to be more complicated than others, that's simply because they consist of several layers of fabric, or many motifs. Once you've learnt the basic technique, you can create any of the designs with ease (and a bit of patience!).

WORKING WITH THE TEMPLATES

The template cards provided with this book feature two versions of each design. One is a full-colour illustration and the other is a technical working diagram, which is a mirror image of the first. This is because with iron-on appliqué the design is traced onto the paper side of the Bondaweb, which is then fused to the wrong side of the fabric. This process requires the template to be reversed so that when the motifs have been fixed in place, they will be the right way round.

Some of the outlines have been re-worked to show how the various elements will be built up to create the final design. Extra fabric has been allowed on some of the shapes: this is represented by dotted lines. You'll also see that some of the fine details have been simplified to make the originals suitable for appliqué.

Many of the templates are used at their actual size, but some will need to be adjusted using a photocopier. A suggested percentage increase or reduction is given in the steps for the individual projects, but you may wish to alter the proportions to suit your own ideas and garment sizes.

1 Trace your motifs directly from the book, or from a photocopy, onto the paper side of the Bondaweb. Leave about 1cm space between the outlines.

2 Snip the individual shapes out roughly around the pencil lines: you don't have to be too precise with your cutting at this stage.

3 Place the motifs, adhesive facing downwards, on the fabric and iron in place. When using printed cotton, make sure you fuse them to the reverse side.

4 Now cut out each of the motifs accurately, following the outline as closely as you can. Use small scissors with sharp blades, to give a clean edge.

5 Peel away the backing paper from each of the motifs, and turn them the right way up. You will be able to feel the rough adhesive layer on the reverse side.

6 Position the motifs on your background and fuse them in place with a cool iron. Use a pressing rather than a sliding action, so that they do not move out of place.

If you are working with felt, always use a handkerchief or piece of muslin as a pressing cloth, so that the heat of the iron doesn't damage and distort the fabric or cause it to stick to your iron.

7 All the motifs are edged with a round of small straight stitches embroidered in a matching or contrasting thread. See how to do this on page 20.

MULTI-COLOURED APPLIQUÉ

The more elaborate designs – like the cowboy and the tea towel roses – are made up from a number of different coloured fabrics. The shapes are built up in layers, starting with the largest elements and finishing with the smallest details.

There are two versions of multi-coloured appliqué: contour appliqué – where the layers stack up one upon the other, much like the lines on a map – and overlapping designs, where some of the pieces, such as leaves, are instead tucked beneath others.

CONTOUR DESIGNS

1 Trace each element of the reversed template onto Bondaweb, following any dotted lines. Cut each shape from fabric, as shown on the previous pages.

2 Peel off the papers and iron down the largest shape. Add the other layers in turn, double-checking their position against the coloured version of the template at the back of the book.

OVERLAPPING DESIGNS

1 Number the small shapes – such as these hooves – as you trace them. Write the corresponding numbers on the template, so they won't get mixed up.

2 The step-by-step instructions for each project will tell you exactly how to build up the finished design, and in which order to go about positioning the various shapes.

OTHER APPLIQUÉ TECHNIQUES

Some fabrics, including fleece, PVC and leather, require a different technique, as they are thicker and cannot be ironed. To appliqué with these materials, you will first need to make a paper pattern for your motifs. The motifs are then sewn on by hand or glued on the background.

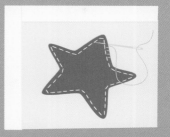

WORKING WITH FLEECE

1 To make a paper pattern, trace and cut out the template following the reversed outline, then turn it over. Pin to your fleece and cut around the edge.

2 Pin the motif to your background material and tack it in place. Remove the pins and work a round of matching straight stitches around the edge, as shown on page 20. Remove the tacking.

WORKING WITH PVC OR OILCLOTH

Pencil around the reversed paper patterns on the back of the cloth and cut around the outline. Arrange the shapes and fix them down with a thin layer of PVA glue.

WORKING WITH LEATHER

It is not easy to sew through more than one layer of leather, so Stanley was redrawn in stencil style. Use a specialised leather needle to stitch down the shapes.

Basic Stitches

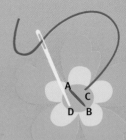

STRAIGHT STITCH

Bring your needle up at A, and take it down again at B, making a short line. Straight stitches in various lengths are used to work details, like facial features, and to 'draw in' small motifs such as this grass.

STRAIGHT STITCH EDGING

Work a round of evenly sized and spaced stitches at right angles to the edge of the appliqué. When worked in matching sewing thread, this gives a subtle finish. Larger stitches in a contrasting thread create a decorative edging.

CROSS STITCH

Work two overlapping straight stitches to form a cross. Work the first stitch from A to B and the second, at a right angle, from C to D. Individual crosses are used as feature stitches or as a decorative way of anchoring tiny appliqué pieces.

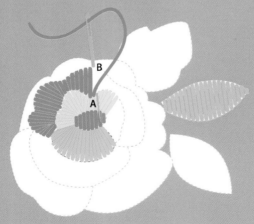

SATIN STITCH

The smooth, shiny finish produced by a row of straight stitches lying side-by-side gives this stitch its name. Work all the stitches in the same direction, from A to B and vary their lengths to fill the shape being worked.

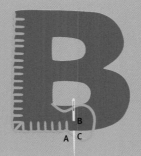

BACKSTITCH

Start with a straight stitch, worked backwards from A to B, then bring the needle up at C, equidistant from B. Make another stitch back to A, and continue in the same way to the end to make a solid line of stitches.

BLANKET STITCH

A traditional finish for woollen blankets, this stitch is used to anchor appliqué or to join two pieces of felt. Start at A, then take the needle down at B and up again, directly below, at C. Pull it through over the thread and repeat to the end.

CHAIN STITCH

This looped stitch produces a wide line suitable for both straight lines and curves. Start at A and loop the thread from left to right. Take the needle back down at A and bring the tip up at B. Pull the needle through over the thread. Repeat this action, starting the next stitch at B.

LAZY DAISY STITCH

These are single chain stitches, where the loop is anchored with a small straight stitch. They can be worked around a central point to make sweet flower motifs. The roses on the cottage tea cosy are made this way.

How to Embroider

HOW TO EMBROIDER

Although the approach to embroidery in this book is very informal, it's worth bearing the following points in mind as you work. You will be investing time and skill in the projects, and it's not difficult to achieve a professional finish.

WORKING WITH EMBROIDERY THREAD

Stranded embroidery thread was used for the embroidery in this book. It comes in looped skeins, held together by a paper band at each end – one wide and one narrow. To avoid tangles, grasp the narrow band with one hand and gently pull the loose thread out from the other end.

CHOOSING A NEEDLE

For embroidery thread, choose a crewel (embroidery) needle. It has a long eye that can accommodate all six strands of stranded embroidery thread and pass easily through the fabric. If you are using sewing thread, you'll need a finer needle with a smaller eye (a 'sharp').

STARTING AND FINISHING

Begin by knotting the end of the thread. If you are working a single line of stitches, pull the needle up through the fabric from the wrong side. For an embroidered design, you need to avoid bumpy knots, so take the needle down on the right side, 2cm from the area to be worked. Your stitches will anchor the surplus thread. Clip off the knot when you have finished. Start the next length of thread by slipping the needle under the back of the existing stitches, leaving a short tail, and securing the thread with a backstitch. Finish off in the same way.

THREADING YOUR NEEDLE

Fold one end of the thread over your needle and hold the loop between finger and thumb. Slide the eye downwards over the loop, then pull the loop through the eye. Work with a 45cm length of thread: any longer and it may fray as you sew.

EMBROIDERING ONTO APPLIQUÉ

Embroidery is useful for the smallest elements of a design, such as the masts on these yachts. Here, a row of blue chain stitch, worked onto the T-shirt, reproduces the cloud outline as it appears on the original design.

EMBROIDERING OVER INTERFACING

This is a great technique for working on stretchy jersey or knitted garments, such as T-shirts or socks, where the fabric has a lot of 'give'. The layer of lightweight non-woven iron-on fusible Vilene interfacing stabilises the background so that the stitches don't distort the fabric. (Remember to trace onto the smooth, non-adhesive side of the interfacing.)

1 The outline motif should match the coloured template, so reverse it on a photocopier if necessary. Trace it onto the interfacing with a fading-ink pen, then cut out carefully. Keep track of the colours by numbering each area on the main template and interfacing.

2 Fuse the motif onto the background, using an iron and a pressing cloth to protect the surface. Fill in each area with satin stitch, worked in the appropriate colour thread – it's as easy as painting by numbers!

TRANSFERRING OUTLINES

If you have a steady hand, you can draw embroidery guidelines directly onto the background fabric. Use a fading-ink pen for most fabrics and a chalk pencil on the very darkest backgrounds. Most of us, however, need a little help.

1 Cut the required shape from a photocopy of the reversed outline template. Turn it over and fit it into the appliqué design, like the last piece of the jigsaw. Draw around the outline with a fading-ink pen or piece of chalk.

2 Embroider along the line using the colour and stitch type given in the step-by-step instructions. Any ink that remains visible will disappear in time.

Kitchen

Some of the very first products I made for my shop were kitchen items. You can't beat a great tea towel to cheer the place up. Whether you want to make an instant gift like an egg cosy, or you're up for something more ambitious, like a hand-appliquéd tablecloth, I hope you will feel inspired!

Linen
Tea Towels

SKILL RATING: 2
WHAT YOU WILL NEED...

- Cotton apron
- Felt: 25cm x 30cm each of red
  and dark red; 10cm x 15cm
  each of light green, dark
  green and white
- Bondaweb
- Iron and pressing cloth
- Sewing thread to match felts
- Sewing workbox (see page 15)

Transform the mundane task of drying up into a
pleasure with these cheery tea towels.

1 For the polka dot towel, use the outline side of the Bubbles
template card to trace 66 circles onto Bondaweb, and cut
them out roughly. Make a temporary ironing board by
covering your work surface with newspapers, topped with
a folded sheet. Iron the circles onto the various fabrics,
ensuring you have a roughly equal number of each colour.
Now cut them out accurately and peel off the backing papers.

2 Lay a tea towel on the 'ironing board' and arrange the
circles across the surface. Iron them in place and edge
each one with a round of matching straight stitches
(see page 20).

3 For the second towel, enlarge the three flowers on the
outline side of the Flowerpot template card by 200%.
For each flower, trace the outline, inner petals and centre
onto Bondaweb, leaving about 5mm around each shape.
Roughly cut out each piece and iron the Bondaweb onto
the fabric using the coloured side of the same template
card as a guide. Cut out along the pencil lines.

4 Iron the largest flower to the centre of one end of a towel, then add its inner petals and
centre. Fuse on the other two flowers on either side and anchor each layer with a round of
straight stitches, using matching sewing thread (see opposite page).

5 With a fading-ink pen, mark the positions of the small dots around the flower centres
where indicated on the template. Using antique white embroidery thread, work the dots in
satin stitch (see page 20).

THE POLKA DOTS WOULD LOOK VERY DIFFERENT IF THEY WERE
CUT FROM PATTERNED FABRICS. WHY NOT TRY MAKING A THIRD
OR EVEN A FOURTH TOWEL?

Napkins &
Placemats

This simple design is a perfect starting point for the appliqué novice!

Cath Kidston

SKILL RATING: 1
WHAT YOU WILL NEED...

- Linen or cotton napkins and placemats
- Bondaweb
- Iron
- Plain cotton fabric for each napkin: 15cm square each of red and green; scrap of brown
- Plain cotton fabric for each placemat: 15cm x 30cm red; 20cm x 30cm green; scrap of brown
- Sewing thread to match fabrics
- Sewing workbox (see page 15)

1 You will find the reversed apple and circle outlines on the Breakfast template card. Enlarge them by 235%, so that the apple is about 10.5cm wide.

2 Using a sharp pencil, trace the apple, highlight, stalk and circles separately onto Bondaweb. You will need one apple and nine circles for each napkin, and four apples and 32 circles per placemat. Cut the shapes out roughly.

3 Iron the apple and the highlight onto either red or green cotton (see opposite), the circles onto green and the stalk onto brown. Cut each shape out around the pencil line and peel off the backing.

4 Fold the napkin into quarters. Place the apple across one corner at an angle, with the top edge facing inwards. Tuck the stalk under the top of the apple. Place the highlight at the top right of the apple. Arrange three green circles in each of the other corners. Iron the shapes in place.

5 If you are making a mat, position the apples the other way up, so that the apple tops face outwards. Arrange them so that the red and green apples lie in opposite corners. Fuse on three green circles in each corner and arrange the others along the edges of the mat.

6 Finish off by working a round of short straight stitches around each shape (see page 20), using matching sewing thread.

THIS TABLE LINEN WAS A LUCKY FIND — IT ALREADY HAD A RED
EDGING. BUT YOU COULD ALWAYS TRIM A PLAIN NAPKIN WITH
BIAS BINDING TO MATCH.

Breakfast Tablecloth

YOU CAN ALTER THE RED AND BLUE COLOUR SCHEME THAT I'VE USED TO CO-ORDINATE WITH YOUR KITCHEN CROCKERY.

Cath Kidston

SKILL RATING: 3
WHAT YOU WILL NEED...

- White cotton tablecloth
- Bondaweb
- Iron
- Plain cotton fabric: scraps of red, navy, egg shell, brown, mustard yellow, white and sage green
- Polka dot fabric: scraps of blue and pink
- Sewing thread to match fabrics
- Sewing workbox (see page 15)

Get your day off to a cheerful start by spreading this appliquéd tablecloth across your breakfast table.

1 Firstly, enlarge the reversed outlines of the cup, bottle and teapot templates on the Breakfast template card by 280%, and the two eggs by 250%.

2 To decide how many motifs you need, make several copies (half of them reversed), cut out the individual shapes and pin them symmetrically around the hem. Remove one at a time as you fill the space with appliqué.

3 Start with a whole egg. Trace the egg and egg cup onto Bondaweb. Iron the egg onto egg shell cotton and the cup onto red or green. Cut out the shapes and remove the papers. Position the cup, tuck the egg under the rim and iron in place.

4 To make the half-eaten egg, follow the dotted lines for the yellow back shell, white yolk and front shell. Position the back shell first, then layer the yolk, front shell and egg cup on top. Iron all the pieces in place.

5 For the teapot, start by ironing on the lid and wide stripes. Then add the narrow polka dot stripes, lapping them over the top edge of the wide ones. Next, add the spout, handle and a dark knob.

6 On the cup and bottle motif, start with the top of the bottle, then add the two pieces of the cap, the bottom outline and shadow. Position the saucer, tuck the saucer rim underneath and iron in place. Position the cup and slip its base underneath. Fuse on and finish off with the dark handle.

7 Secure each motif with a round of straight stitches around the edge (see page 20), using matching sewing thread.

THIS PROJECT IS TRULY A LABOUR OF LOVE. IF YOUR TIME IS LIMITED, DECORATE JUST A SINGLE CORNER, OR MAYBE THE CENTRAL PART OF YOUR TABLECLOTH.

Strawberry Apron

IF YOU DON'T WANT POCKETS, SIMPLY CUT THE STRAWBERRIES WITH A BONDAWEB BACKING AND IRON THEM DIRECTLY ONTO THE APRON, USING A PRESSING CLOTH.

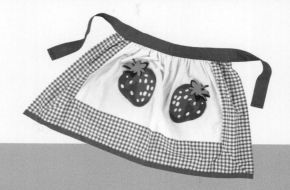

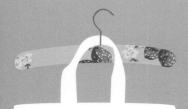

Cath Kidston

SKILL RATING: 2
WHAT YOU WILL NEED...

- Cotton apron
- Felt: 25cm x 30cm each of red and dark red; 10cm x 15cm each of light green, dark green and white
- Bondaweb
- Iron and pressing cloth
- Sewing thread to match felts
- Sewing workbox (see page 15)

Even the most reluctant cook will feel like a domestic goddess in this pretty pinny.

1 To make the strawberry pockets, enlarge the outline on the Strawberry template card by 120%, so that it is about 19cm tall (including the stem). Cut the photocopy out around the outside edge to make a paper template. Pin this onto the red felt and cut out carefully around the edge.

2 Trace the dark red shadows onto Bondaweb following the dotted line, cut them out roughly and iron onto dark red felt. Always use a pressing cloth when ironing felt. Cut out accurately and position on the red strawberry. Secure with a round of red straight stitches around the edge (see page 20).

3 Make the hull and stalk from light and dark green felt and the seeds from white felt. Fuse them in place with the iron, remembering the pressing cloth. Anchor each piece with a round of straight stitches, using matching sewing thread.

4 Now make a reversed copy of the enlarged template and put the second pocket together in the same way, as a mirror image of the first.

5 Pin the pockets on the apron, making sure they are level. Secure with red straight stitches, all around the berry from 2cm away from the green hull on the left to 2cm away from the hull on the right. Make a few extra stitches at each side of the opening to reinforce it.

IF YOU ARE A KEEN SEAMSTRESS, YOU COULD MAKE YOUR OWN APRON FROM A RECTANGLE OF PLAIN FABRIC TRIMMED WITH A GINGHAM BORDER.

Egg
Cosies

Keep your boiled eggs
warm in traditional style with
a trio of adorable felt cosies.

1 First make the cosy pattern, by folding the paper in half lengthways. Draw a curve across one top corner, cut along the line and open out. Using this as a guide, cut two shapes – a front and a back – from red, blue and pink felt.

2 For the red cosy, trace the largest star outline on the Stars template card onto Bondaweb and fuse it onto pink felt with an iron – make sure you always use a pressing cloth when working with felt. Cut around the line, peel off the paper and fuse the star onto a red felt shape. Work straight stitches around the edge (see page 20), using green embroidery thread.

3 To make the blue cosy, enlarge the single rose outline on the left of the Songbird template card by 115% and trace the elements onto Bondaweb. Cut them out and fix the petals to the appropriate felt, using the photograph as a guide.

4 Remove the backings and centre the main rose on a blue felt cosy piece. Tuck the leaves under each side, add the petals and iron them on. Straight stitch around each piece of felt with matching sewing thread. Embroider the centre of the rose in straight stitch (page 20) using brown stranded thread.

Cath Kidston

SKILL RATING: 1
WHAT YOU WILL NEED...

- 7cm x 9cm rectangle of paper
- Ruler
- Bondaweb
- Iron and pressing cloth
- Felt: 12cm x 20cm pink; 12cm x 15cm red; 12cm x 15cm blue; scraps of light green, dark green, white and brown
- Embroidery thread in green, brown, antique white, red and pink
- Sewing thread to match felts
- Sewing workbox (see page 15)

5 For the pink cosy, reduce the small strawberry outline on the Strawberry template card to 60%. Using Bondaweb, make the berry from red felt, then add the hull in light and dark green. Work the seeds in tiny straight stitches, using antique white.

6 To finish the cosies, pin the fronts to the matching backs. Tack together, leaving the bottom open, then join with blanket stitch (see page 21): green for the red cosy, pink for the blue and red for the pink cosy.

Tea
Cosy

Teatime isn't complete without a cosy sitting on the teapot – so I have used the red cockerel from my Breakfast fabric to jolly up this plain polka-dot version.

SKILL RATING: 2
WHAT YOU WILL NEED...

- Ready-made tea cosy
- Bondaweb
- Felt: 20cm square of red; 10cm square each of white and dark green; scraps of light blue, yellow and brown
- Iron and pressing cloth
- Sewing thread to match felts
- 1 small button, for the eye
- Sewing workbox (see page 15)

1 Enlarge the cockerel outline on the Breakfast template card by 210%, or to fit your cosy. Trace the main outline (omitting the feet, coxcomb and wattle) onto Bondaweb. Cut out roughly and fuse onto red felt with an iron. Always use a pressing cloth when working with felt. Cut carefully around the pencil line. Peel off the backing paper and iron the cockerel to the centre of the tea cosy.

2 The details are all made with Bondaweb in the same way. Draw around the outside edge of the wing and cut this shape from white felt. Iron it in place, then add the green layer on top. Next add the three white feathers and the smaller blue feathers so the bird has more of a three-dimensional look.

3 Fuse on the six white tail feathers, adding two green and two blue feathers on top. Cut the foot, coxcomb and wattle from yellow felt and iron them in place. These three pieces butt up to the main shape, without overlapping. Add the two brown shadow pieces, which fit inside the edge of the cockerel's body.

4 Secure each piece with short straight stitches (see page 20), using matching sewing thread.

5 The finishing touch, which gives real character to this design, is the eye – a small white button sewn on with dark thread.

Framed
Flowerpot

DRAW THE SCALLOPED EDGE OF THE TABLECLOTH ONTO GRAPH PAPER, TRACING AROUND A COIN OR LARGE BUTTON TO CREATE THE SHALLOW CURVES.

Cath Kidston

SKILL RATING: 3
WHAT YOU WILL NEED...

- Picture frame
- Thick cream fabric to fit the frame
- Bondaweb, iron and pressing cloth
- Cotton fabric: 30cm x 45cm red gingham; 10cm x 15cm each of plain green and blue polka dot
- Felt: 10cm x 30cm red; 10cm square each of blue, pink and yellow; 4cm x 15cm brown
- Sewing thread to match fabrics
- Red embroidery thread
- 3 buttons; 4 red beads; 3 diamantés
- Sewing workbox (see page 15)

Give new life to an old picture frame with this appliqué flower pot adapted from my Circus Flowers fabric.

1 To make the 'tablecloth', cut two 5cm strips of Bondaweb to the same width as the cream background. Iron them onto gingham: one parallel to the checks, the other at right angles. Peel off the papers.

2 Iron the first strip to the background, 2cm from the bottom. Fuse on the second strip directly above. Draw a 1.5cm scalloped band, of the same width, onto Bondaweb, cut it from red felt and iron it on over the join. Remember to use a pressing cloth with felt.

3 Increase the size of the outline on the Flowerpot template card to fit within your frame. Trace the two parts of the flowerpot onto Bondaweb and cut out roughly. Press the main pot onto blue felt and the rim onto brown. Cut out and fuse onto the backing. Add six red felt dots to the main pot.

4 Cut out the leaves and flowers from felt and fabric in the same way, using the picture opposite as a colour guide. Peel off the backings.

5 Layer the pieces, putting the blue and yellow petals in position, then adding the pink flower with its red centre to the right. Tuck the leaves under the edge of the flowers as shown and add the three red petals and the blue flower centre. Press all the pieces in place.

6 Edge each shape with straight stitches (see page 20), using matching sewing thread. Embroider red blanket stitch (see page 21) around the largest flower centre and the dots. Add a button to each flower centre, four red beads to the yellow petals and three diamantés to the very top.

THE GINGHAM TABLECLOTH IS SKILFULLY CUT ON THE BIAS OF THE FABRIC TO CREATE THE ILLUSION OF PERSPECTIVE.

Pot Holders
& Oven Gloves

MY POT HOLDERS CAME EDGED IN PINK. ADD YOUR OWN BINDING IF YOURS ARE PLAIN, OR CHANGE THE COLOUR TO MATCH YOUR FABRIC CHOICE.

Add a touch of retro domesticity to your kitchen with these pretty, practical accessories.

Cath Kidston

SKILL RATING: 2
WHAT YOU WILL NEED...

- 2 oven gloves and 2 pot holders
- Bondaweb
- Iron and pressing cloth
- Felt: 10cm x 20cm egg shell
- Plain cotton fabric: scraps of white, yellow and brown
- Cotton fabric prints: 15cm x 20cm pink polka dot; 10cm square of blue polka dot; 10cm x 15cm floral
- Sewing thread to match fabrics
- Dressmaker's fading-ink pen
- Embroidery thread in brown
- Sewing workbox (see page 15)

1 Adjust the egg cup outlines on the Breakfast template card to fit the oven gloves: mine were enlarged by 325%. Trace the various parts of the template onto Bondaweb and cut out each shape roughly. Fuse the shells onto felt (remember to use a pressing cloth when working with felt) and the other shapes onto cotton fabric: white for the yolk and highlights, yellow for the inner shell, polka dots for the egg cups and brown for the bottom rims. Cut out carefully.

2 Remove the papers and position the two egg cups on the gloves. Tuck the shells and rims under them, then add the inner shell and yolk to the half-eaten egg. Iron in place. Finish off with the three small highlights. Secure each piece with straight stitches (see page 20), using matching sewing thread.

3 Enlarge the teacup motif by 260% to fit a 21cm pot holder. Trace the cup and its rim, the saucer and its rim, and the handle onto Bondaweb. Cut out carefully. Iron the cup and saucer to the back of the polka-dot and floral prints, and the other pieces to the brown fabric. Cut out carefully.

4 Peel off the backings and place the cup and saucer on the pot holder. Slip the brown rims in place, add the handle, and iron in place. To make a mirror image on the second holder, reverse the handle template and fuse it on at the other side of the cup.

5 Mark the five steam lines above the cup with a fading-ink pen. Chain stitch over these curves (see page 21), using brown embroidery thread.

ADD A USEFUL TAPE LOOP TO YOUR GLOVES AND POT HOLDERS IF THE MANUFACTURERS HAVEN'T PROVIDED ONE, SO YOU CAN HANG THEM UP NEXT TO THE STOVE.

Bedroom

I love these pillowcases covered in appliquéd spots, and it's a great way to use up scraps of fabric. It's easy to pick up vintage bed linen at flea markets, otherwise, basic bedding is now very cheap on the high street.

Rose
Shawl

THE SHELL PINK SHAWL GIVES A VERY FEMININE LOOK TO THIS PROJECT. TO MAKE A STRONGER IMPACT, USE A DARKER BACKGROUND COLOUR.

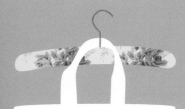

Cath Kidston

SKILL RATING: 3
WHAT YOU WILL NEED...

- Pink woollen throw or pashmina
- Bondaweb
- Iron and pressing cloth
- Plain cotton fabric: 15cm x 20cm each of pink, red, light green and dark brown
- Sewing thread to match fabrics
- Sewing workbox (see page 15)

Transform your bedroom into a boudoir with a luxurious rose-strewn shawl.

1 Trace the two main rose outlines from the Antique Rose template card onto the Bondaweb, following the dotted line at the edge of the smaller flower. Cut them out roughly. Fuse the large rose onto pink cotton and the small one onto red cotton. Cut them out accurately.

2 Peel away the papers and position the roses in the centre at the end of the shawl. Tuck the left edge of the red rose under the pink rose.

3 Now trace all 12 leaves onto Bondaweb, following the dotted and unbroken lines. Iron the adhesive side onto the green fabric.

4 For the next stage, start at the centre top and work clockwise. Cut out the large double leaf, take off the paper backing and slip it behind the two roses. Position the other leaves, using the coloured motif on the same template card as a guide.

5 Lay a pressing cloth over the pieces to protect the shawl from direct heat and fuse them on with a warm iron.

6 Sew a round of short straight stitches around each rose and leaf (see page 20), using matching sewing thread.

7 Trace all the red petals for the pink rose and iron the Bondaweb pieces onto red cotton. Cut out and iron on one petal at a time, double-checking the positions against the template. Make the shadows from brown cotton in the same way.

8 Add the pink petals and brown shadows to the red rose, then straight stitch around the edge of the shape in pink, red or brown thread.

I ENLARGED THE TEMPLATE JUST SLIGHTLY TO FIT MY SHAWL, BUT YOU COULD INCREASE THE TEMPLATE BY 200% FOR A REALLY DRAMATIC LOOK.

Hot Water Bottle Cover

Snuggle up to a fleecy version of Stanley!

Cath Kidston

SKILL RATING: 2
WHAT YOU WILL NEED...

- Red fleece hot water bottle cover
- Sharp pencil and tracing paper
- Fleece fabric: 25cm square
  of light stone; 10cm x 20cm
  dark stone; scrap of red fleece
  for collar
- Sewing thread to match fabrics
- Small button, for dog tag
- Dressmaker's fading-ink pen
- Embroidery thread in brown
- Sewing workbox (see page 15)

1 Trace the Stanley outline on the Stanley template card onto paper. Cut out his head and body, then turn the pieces over so that he faces to the right. Pin the two shapes to the light stone fleece and cut them out.

2 Position Stanley on the front of the cover, leaving a narrow gap between his head and body. Pin the shapes in place (making sure the pins don't go through the back), and tack them in position. Edge each shape with straight stitches (see page 20), using matching sewing thread.

3 Now cut out the markings on Stanley's body and leg from the paper template, turn them over and pin them onto the dark stone fleece. Cut out, then pin, tack and sew them in place, using dark stone thread.

4 For Stanley's collar, cut a 5mm strip of red felt or fleece to fit across his neck. Tack it in place, then sew in place with red straight stitches. Sew a button at the centre for the dog tag.

5 Draw on the eyes, nose and mouth with a dressmaker's fading-ink pen and embroider over the lines in satin and straight stitches, using brown embroidery thread. Cut the inner ears from scraps of dark stone fleece and sew them on with matching sewing thread.

6 Use the bone on outline on the same card to make an appliqué motif in light stone felt and sew it to the flap with straight stitches.

YOU'LL FIND IT EASIER TO SEW THE SHAPES ONTO THE COVER
IF YOU PUT ONE HAND INSIDE THE COVER TO SUPPORT THE
FABRIC WHILST YOU STITCH WITH THE OTHER HAND.

Spotty Sheet & Pillowcase

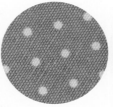

IF YOU LIKE THIS PROJECT, THEN YOU COULD TRY IT WITH A DIFFERENT MOTIF – PERHAPS THE SHOOTING STARS FOR A NIGHT-TIME THEME?

Cath Kidston

SKILL RATING: 1
WHAT YOU WILL NEED...

- Cotton pillowcase and sheet
- Bondaweb
- Old newspapers and a spare sheet
- Iron
- Cotton fabrics: scraps of selection of prints
- Sewing thread to match fabrics
- Sewing workbox (see page 15)

Embellishing bedlinen is a brilliant way of using up tiny odd scraps of cotton fabric.

1 Gather together all your fabric scraps and launder any new pieces. Decide on two colours for your main theme – I went for pink and blue – and pick out a selection of patterned cottons in these shades.

2 Trace the 20 circle outlines on the Bubbles template card onto the paper side of the Bondaweb, using a sharp pencil. The pillowcase uses one hundred circles, so you will need to trace the page five times. Cut out each of the circles roughly, leaving a border of about 5mm around each one.

3 Protect your table with a thick layer of opened-out newspapers covered by a spare folded sheet: this will be your temporary ironing board. Iron the dots onto the wrong side of the various fabrics, choosing the most interesting areas of the printed designs, and cut out along the pencil lines.

4 Spread out your pillowcase on the sheet. Peel off the backing papers and arrange the circles randomly across the pillowcase with the adhesive side downwards. Press them in place with a warm iron.

5 Edge each circle with straight stitches (see page 20 and detail on opposite page), using matching sewing thread.

6 The edge of the sheet is decorated in the same way. For a narrow border, as shown, cut about 70 circles for a double sheet and about 40 for a single sheet.

IF YOU DON'T WANT TO COVER THE PILLOWCASE COMPLETELY, USE FEWER CIRCLES AND ARRANGE THEM AS A BORDER OR IN A SIMPLE REPEATING PATTERN.

Songbird
Bed Socks

YOUR BED SOCKS WILL REQUIRE SPECIAL AFTERCARE. ALWAYS WASH THEM GENTLY WITH SOAPFLAKES IN COOL WATER, RINSE WELL AND DRY THEM FLAT.

Cath Kidston

SKILL RATING: 3
WHAT YOU WILL NEED...

- Pair of cashmere socks
- Lightweight non-woven iron-on interfacing
- Dressmaker's fading-ink pen
- Iron and pressing cloth
- Embroidery thread in light brown, red, pink, dark brown, antique white and green
- Sewing workbox (see page 15)

These pretty bed socks are a real luxury and will keep your feet toasty warm all winter.

1 Enlarge the bird outline on the right of the Songbird template card by 120%. Place a 5cm x 6cm rectangle of interfacing over the outline with the smooth (non-adhesive) upwards. Use a fading-ink pen to draw over the lines, then snip the bird out around the outside edge.

2 Iron the cut-out bird to the side of one sock, just below the ribbing. Use a very cool iron and remember your pressing cloth to protect the soft fibres.

3 Thread a large-eyed needle with light brown embroidery thread. Embroider the bird's wings in three bands of satin stitch (see page 20), working between the ink lines. Next work the tail, body and head, also in satin stitch. Look carefully at the photograph to check the colours and direction of the stitches.

4 Add the pink markings on the head in satin stitch, then work a few short stitches in dark brown for the eye, beak and leg.

5 Finish off by filling in the rest of the head with white satin stitch and using the rest of the thread to work backstitch (see page 21) across the neck and between the body, tail and wing. Work the branch in green backstitch.

6 Embroider a second bird on the other sock, reversing the image so that you have a matching pair.

SLIP ONE HAND INTO THE TOP OF THE SOCK TO SUPPORT THE FABRIC AS YOU EMBROIDER WITH THE OTHER — BUT TRY NOT TO PRICK YOUR FINGERS!

Detailed
Pillowcases

THE FRILLY EDGING ON
THESE PILLOWCASES
COMPLEMENTS THE
DELICATE FLOWERS,
BUT THEY WOULD WORK
EQUALLY WELL WITH A
PLAIN BORDER.

Cath Kidston

SKILL RATING: 2
WHAT YOU WILL NEED...

- Pair of laundered pillowcases
- Bondaweb
- Iron
- Plain cotton fabric: scraps of pink, red, white, brown, green, yellow, orange, blue and dark red
- Sewing thread to match fabrics
- Embroidery thread to match fabrics
- Sewing workbox (see page 15)

Sweet dreams are guaranteed when you fall asleep on a flower-strewn pillow.

1 The two floral corner outlines are on the Circus Flowers template card. I used them this size, but you can enlarge them slightly for a bolder look.

2 Trace the various elements onto Bondaweb, following the dotted lines on the larger flowers. Number each part of the design, then copy these numbers onto your tracing.

3 Cut out all the flowers, leaves and dots roughly and iron them onto the cotton fabrics. Refer to the coloured diagram on the same template card for the right shades.

4 Trim each piece around the pencil line, but don't peel off the paper until you are ready to iron it in place: this way you can keep track of the numbering system.

5 The largest flower is the foundation for each flower grouping, so position this first, then position the two layers of petals and the dark centre on top. Fix them in place with a warm iron, then add the smaller flowers and their centres. Finally, arrange the coloured dots and the leaves around the flowers and fuse in place.

6 Straight stitch around the edge of each large shape (see page 20), using matching sewing thread. Using embroidery threads, decorate the leaves with a single dark green straight stitch down the centre, and the dots and flower centres with a simple cross stitch (see page 20), using matching threads.

THE CIRCUS FLOWER DESIGNS LOOK GOOD ON A LARGE OR SMALL SCALE: TAKE A LOOK AT THE TEA TOWEL ON PAGE 26 TO SEE THE SUPER-SIZED VERSION.

Flower-trimmed
Pyjamas

IF YOUR PYJAMAS DON'T HAVE A
POCKET, YOU COULD EMBROIDER
THE ROW OF FLOWERS DIRECTLY
ONTO THE JACKET.

SKILL RATING: 2
WHAT YOU WILL NEED...

- Pair of cotton pyjamas
- Lightweight non-woven iron-on interfacing
- Dressmaker's fading-ink pen
- Iron and pressing cloth
- Embroidery thread in pink, red and antique white
- Sewing workbox (see page 15)

Red and pink embroidered flowers add a sweet, girly touch to a classic pair of cotton pyjamas.

1 You'll find the templates for this project on the Basket of Flowers template card. Adjust the size so that they fit your pyjamas: I reduced them both to 70% of the original.

2 Cut a strip of iron-on interfacing slightly larger than the row of flowers. Lay it over the photocopy with the smooth (non-adhesive) side upwards. Trace the outlines with a fading-ink pen, then cut out the five flowers.

3 Fuse the flowers to the top of the pocket, with a cool iron – use a pressing cloth. Iron on the central large flower first, with the smooth side still upward, then position a small one on each side and another large one at each end of the row.

4 The embroidery is worked in satin stitch (see page 20). Sew the petals first in either red or pink, angling each block of stitches towards the centre, then work the flower centre in the other colour.

5 Decorate the collar with the two sprigs, positioned so that the buds point inwards. Embroider the flowers as before, in red with pink centres, and work the bud in pink satin stitch.

6 Stitch the leaves in antique white satin stitch, and work a single straight stitch down the centre (see page 20). Embellish the trousers by adding another sprig to the outer hems.

IF YOU LIKE THIS TYPE OF EMBROIDERY, TRY WORKING AN ELEGANT MONOGRAM ON ANOTHER PAIR OF PYJAMAS: YOU'LL FIND A FULL ALPHABET ON THE ALPHABET TEMPLATE CARD.

Country
Cottage Cushion

Cath Kidston

SKILL RATING: 3
WHAT YOU WILL NEED...

- 45cm square cushion cover
- Bondaweb
- Iron and pressing cloth
- Tweed: 10cm x 25cm each of pink and red; scrap of brown
- Felt: 10cm x 20cm brown; 10cm square each of green and stone; scraps of blue, yellow, white and red
- Gingham: 10cm square
- Sewing thread to match fabrics
- Embroidery thread in blue, antique white, brown, green, pink and red
- Sewing workbox (see page 15)

A new take on an old favourite: this cushion cover will add a little touch of period country charm to your bedroom.

1 Enlarge the template on the Country Cottage template card by 135%. Trace the cottage and the roof onto Bondaweb. Iron the cottage to pink tweed and the roof to red tweed. Cut out and peel off the backing. Fuse to the centre of the cover, so the roof overlaps the cottage. Add the chimney in red and brown tweed.

2 For each window, cut the outer squares from brown felt, the inner squares from blue, and the curtains from gingham. Remove the papers, then iron on the brown squares, the blue squares and the curtains. Anchor the brown felt and the curtains with a ring of straight stitches (see page 20), using matching sewing thread. Use blue embroidery thread to outline the inner edge of the curtains. Work two long straight stitches in white and brown for each window frame and anchor the centres with small diagonal stitches.

3 Cut out the felt details: green grass and hedges; brown porch, gate and doorknob; stone path; yellow door; white fanlight and cloud. The wall is red tweed. Peel off the papers and position as follows: grass, path, porch, door, doorknob, fanlight, gate, wall and hedges. Press and stitch in place.

4 Draw the lines for the climbing roses, blue cloud and birds with a fading-ink pen. Embroider the roses in chain, lazy daisy and straight stitches, the cloud in chain stitch and the birds in straight stitch, using appropriate colours (see pages 20–21). Complete the fanlight with brown straight stitches. Embroider the door knob. Finally, make eight dots from red felt and two brown bricks, fuse to the hedge and wall, then add the leaves in straight stitch.

Bags

I am a bag addict, not expensive designer 'it' bags, but great everyday shopping bags – there is nothing like a canvas tote. Take your pick of our designs to customise a dull-looking bag with stars, cowboys or classic rose prints. You'll be spoilt for choice!

Flowery Tote

Cath Kidston

SKILL RATING: 1
WHAT YOU WILL NEED...

- Cotton tote bag
- Bondaweb
- Iron
- Polka dot cotton fabric: small
  amount each of dark blue,
  light blue, pink, green, red and
  yellow
- Small scissors/nail scissors
- Sewing thread to match fabrics
- Sewing workbox (see page 15)

Transform a plain tote bag into an eco-friendly shopper by adding a scattering of spotty flowers.

1 Enlarge the reversed flower outline on the Flowers template card by 120%. Trace the outlines and centre circles onto the paper side of the Bondaweb. I used 25 flowers, so traced the whole page twice, then added an extra bloom.

2 Cut out the flowers roughly, leaving a border of about 5mm around each one. With the adhesive side facing downwards, iron them onto the back of the various fabrics.

3 Now cut the flowers out carefully around the outside edge. Snip out the centre circles and peel off all the backing papers.

4 Lay the bag out on your ironing board and spread the flowers across the front. When you are happy with your arrangement, fuse them in place.

5 Decorate the inside and outside edges of each bloom with a round of straight stitches (see page 20), using matching sewing thread.

SHARP NAIL SCISSORS WITH CURVED BLADES ARE IDEAL FOR CUTTING OUT THE TINY FLOWER CENTRES.

Shiny Flowers
Cosmetic Bag

Cath Kidston

SKILL RATING: 1
WHAT YOU WILL NEED...

- White zip-up cosmetic bag
- Thin PVC fabric: 8cm square of light blue; 10cm x 15cm red
- Glue stick
- Sewing thread in red and blue
- Sewing workbox (see page 15)

The design on this PVC bag is floral without being fussy. You'll find that sewing with plastic fabrics is no more difficult than working with cotton or felt.

1 Enlarge the flower templates at the foot of the Basket of Flowers template card so that they fit your bag. Mine was 13cm deep so I increased the size by 200%. Cut out one large and one small flower from your photocopy to use as a paper pattern.

2 Place the large flower on the reverse side of the red PVC and draw around it twice. Draw around the small flower once, on the back of the blue fabric.

3 Now cut the round flower centre from the paper pattern. Draw around the large one twice on the blue fabric and the small one once on the red PVC. Cut all the shapes out around the pencil lines.

4 Fix the blue flower to the centre of the bag using a small amount of adhesive from the glue stick. Add one red flower on each side, keeping the centres on the same level. Now glue the flower centres in place.

5 Secure the appliqué shapes by working a round of straight stitches around the edge of each one (see page 20), using either red or blue sewing thread.

USE A 'SHARP' NEEDLE TO SEW DOWN THE FLOWERS AND
ENSURE THAT YOU STITCH THROUGH THE BAG ONLY — NOT THE
BULKY LINING.

Starry
Tote

IF YOU CAN'T FIND PVC FABRIC, YOU COULD CUT THE STARS FROM WHITE COTTON FABRIC AND USE THE IRON-ON APPLIQUÉ TECHNIQUE TO FIX THEM TO THE BAG.

Cath Kidston

SKILL RATING: 1
WHAT YOU WILL NEED...

- Red tote bag
- Thin PVC fabric: 30cm x 40cm white
- Newspaper
- PVA adhesive
- Paintbrush
- Sewing workbox (see page 15)

Keep this sparkling tote folded up in your handbag and you'll never need a plastic carrier again!

1 Photocopy the outline on the Stars template card and cut out five different-sized stars. Alternatively, you can trace them onto tracing paper.

2 Using a sharp pencil, draw around the paper stars on the back of the PVC 35 times, making sure you have a roughly equal number of each one. You may need to make more stars if your bag is larger than mine, which measures 35 x 40cm.

3 Fold the newspaper so that it is the same size as your bag, then slip it inside. Place the bag on your work surface and arrange the stars across the front, shiny side up.

4 Stick each star down with a light coating of PVA. Paint the glue over the back and wait until the surface feels tacky, rather than wet. Turn the star over and smooth it in place, pressing each point down with your fingertips.

CUT TWICE AS MANY STARS IF YOU WANT TO COVER BOTH SIDES OF YOUR BAG, BUT BE SURE TO LET THE GLUE DRY ON ONE SIDE BEFORE STARTING THE OTHER SIDE.

Cowboy
Canvas Bag

Cath Kidston

SKILL RATING: 3
WHAT YOU WILL NEED...

- Canvas bag
- Bondaweb
- Iron and pressing cloth
- Felt: 20cm square of light stone; 5cm x 10cm square each of dark stone, warm brown and peat brown
- Woven fabric: scraps of red tweed, gingham and denim
- Sewing thread to match fabrics
- Embroidery thread in red and brown
- Dressmaker's fading-ink pen
- Sewing workbox (see page 15)

The vintage cowboy rides again! This time on a roomy canvas bag, complete with a western leather trim.

1 Enlarge the cowboy outline on the Cowboy template card to fit your bag, then trace him and his horse onto Bondaweb. Cut out roughly and fuse to light stone felt. Leave the backing paper on as you add the other pieces and remember your pressing cloth when ironing felt.

2 First dress the cowboy in a red tweed shirt, gingham kerchief and blue jeans (remember the Bondaweb goes on the back of the fabrics).

3 Use dark stone felt for the saddle, and the shadowed areas on the horse and Stetson. The boot, saddle strap and holster are cut from warm brown felt, with an extra detail on the holster in red tweed.

4 For the final layer, make the hooves, mane, bridle, and the cowboy's hair from peat brown felt. Now you can peel off the backing.

5 Anchor each piece to the main motif with straight stitches (see page 20), using matching sewing thread. Sew along only the inside edges of the shapes and around the details that fit within the outline (e.g., the boot and bridle) as the outside edge of the motif will be stitched to the bag.

6 Iron the finished motif in place on the front of the bag. Straight stitch all around the edge, using the appropriate colour thread. Be careful not to stitch through the lining, if your bag has one.

7 Draw in the lasso with a fading-ink pen and work over the line in chain stitch (see page 21), using red embroidery thread. Add tiny stitches in brown embroidery thread for the features on both horse and cowboy.

Embroidered Evening Purse

Cath Kidston

SKILL RATING: 3
WHAT YOU WILL NEED...

- Fabric purse
- Dressmaker's fading-ink pen
- Lightweight non-woven iron-on interfacing
- Iron and pressing cloth
- Embroidery thread in pink, red, antique white, green and brown
- 5cm square of fabric to match purse, for covering button
- 2cm self-cover button
- Sewing workbox (see page 15)

Just the right size for your essentials, this purse makes a charming accessory for an evening out.

1 You will find the outline for the rose swag on the Antique Rose template card. Check the size against your bag and adjust it on a photocopier if necessary.

2 Using a fading-ink pen, trace your chosen flowers and larger leaves onto iron-on interfacing. Cut them out carefully.

3 Position the motifs symmetrically around the flap, setting aside the centre rose for the button and leaving a space for it. Iron them in place, using a pressing cloth. Fuse the rose to the centre of the fabric square.

4 Mark in the stalks and smaller leaves with a fading-ink pen to complete the swag.

5 Start by working the pink parts of the roses in satin stitch (see page 20), then add the red petals. Work the flower centres in antique white straight stitches (see page 20).

6 Embroider the leaves in green thread and add a brown straight stitch to the centre of each. Work the stems in green backstitch (see page 21).

7 Embroider the centre rose in the same way, then cover the button according to the manufacturer's instructions. Sew it securely in place to complete the swag design.

YOU COULD LOOK OUT FOR A BEAUTIFUL VINTAGE BUTTON TO USE AS AN ALTERNATIVE TO THE EMBROIDERED FASTENING.

Floral
Holdall

THE BRIGHT RED FLOWERS, WITH THEIR SHINY WHITE CENTRES, GIVE REAL VIBRANCY TO A PLAIN GREEN BAG, BUT A MULTI-COLOURED SELECTION WOULD LOOK EVEN MORE DAZZLING.

Cath Kidston

SKILL RATING: 1
WHAT YOU WILL NEED...

- Plain sports bag, 50cm wide
- A4 sheet of thin card
- Ballpoint pen
- Nylon fabric: 50cm x 80cm red
- PVC fabric: 15cm x 25cm white
- PVA adhesive and paintbrush
- Sewing workbox (see page 15)

If you pack your sports kit in this flowery holdall, a trip to the gym will become an uplifting event!

1 Choose five different flower outlines from the Flowers template card. Photocopy them onto card, enlarging the size by 120%. Cut out around the edge and snip out the centres.

2 Draw around the inside and outside of the templates, directly onto the back of the red fabric. I used 45 flowers – nine of each size – on my bag, but you may need more for a larger holdall.

3 Now cut a circle of white PVC, about 2cm in diameter, to make a centre for each flower.

4 Paint a thin layer of glue on the back of the first flower, just around the centre hole. When it is almost dry, press a white circle, shiny side downwards, onto the glue. Do the same with the other flowers.

5 When the PVA has set, you can glue the flowers in place. Lay them, face down, on newspaper and coat the entire back with a thin layer of PVA. Leave it until tacky, then press the flowers down firmly onto the bag, petal by petal. Start at the ends. Fix one flower to the centre then surround it with a ring of five more. The other flowers are arranged around the main bag, in the space between the straps.

6 When you have finished, double-check all the flowers and glue down any areas that may have lifted.

TO GET THE WHITE CENTRAL PIECES THE RIGHT SIZE, DRAW AROUND A BOTTLE TOP OR LARGE COIN.

Strawberry Basket

THE FELT MOTIF ECHOES THE
BRIGHT STRAWBERRY PRINT
LINING. CHOOSE AN OVER-SIZED
FLOWER TO DECORATE A BASKET
WITH A FLORAL LINING.

Cath Kidston

SKILL RATING: 2
WHAT YOU WILL NEED...

- Cotton-lined basket
- Bondaweb
- Iron and pressing cloth
- Felt: 20cm square each of light
  red and dark red; 10cm x 15cm
  white; 10cm square each of dark
  green and light green
- Sewing thread to match felts
- Glue stick
- Embroidery thread in light green
  and red
- Sewing workbox (see page 15)

This useful basket, with its bold motif and patterned lining, embodies my love of vintage style given a contemporary twist.

1 The reversed strawberry outlines are on the Strawberry template card. I used the largest one for this project and increased its size just slightly to 110%, so that it looked in the right proportion to the basket.

2 Trace right around the motif (including the hull) onto Bondaweb and cut it out 5mm from the edge. Fuse onto the light red felt using an iron. Always use a pressing cloth when working with felt. Cut out the strawberry accurately.

3 Now trace the outline for the dark red felt, following the dotted lines where the hull overlaps. Peel off the backing and iron to the main shape.

4 Cut the dark and light green hull pieces and iron them onto the strawberry. Finally, make the seeds from white felt and fuse them in place.

5 Peel the backing paper from the main shape and straight stitch (see page 20) around the seeds and along the inside edges of the dark red felt and the hull, using matching sewing thread. You don't need to stitch around the outside edge of the motif.

6 Position the finished motif centrally on one side of the basket, holding it in place with a few dabs from a glue stick. Straight stitch in place, using green or red embroidery thread. Sew through the basket with a stabbing action, taking care not to catch the lining.

A ROW OF THE THREE SMALLER STRAWBERRIES WOULD MAKE A GOOD ALTERNATIVE DECORATION FOR THIS RECTANGULAR BASKET.

Rose
Knitting Bag

YOU COULD CREATE A DIFFERENT-COLOURED ROSE ON THE OTHER SIDE OF THE BAG, SO IT WILL GO WITH ANY COLOUR SCHEME.

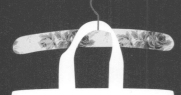

Cath Kidston

SKILL RATING: 3
WHAT YOU WILL NEED...

- Knitting bag
- Bondaweb
- Iron and pressing cloth
- Tweed: 20cm square each of pink, red and brown
- Sewing thread to match tweeds
- Dressmaker's fading-ink pen
- Embroidery thread in brown
- Sewing workbox (see page 15)

Now that knitting is once again fashionable, you will need a suitable bag in which to keep your work.

1 The reversed outline motif for this project is on the Antique Rose template card. I used it at the given size for my bag, but you may wish to make it larger.

2 Start by tracing the two roses onto Bondaweb. Cut the shapes out roughly and iron them onto the pink and red tweed using a pressing cloth. Cut out accurately, remove the backing and position them on the bag, tucking the red rose under the edge of the pink one.

3 Now trace the leaves ignoring the vein lines. You might find it helps to number each one as you draw it and mark these numbers on the outline, as they all look quite similar.

4 Peel the paper from each leaf in turn and arrange them around the roses. Tuck some of them under the edges of the roses, where indicated by the dotted lines. Iron the flowers and leaves to the bag, using a pressing cloth.

5 Next add red tweed petals to the pink rose and pink tweed petals to the red rose. Once again you'll find it helpful to number them as you work. Sew around each shape in straight stitch (see page 20), using matching sewing thread.

6 The brown petal detail is embroidered. Referring to the coloured template, draw the shapes in with a fading-ink pen, then work over them in satin stitch (see page 20), using brown embroidery thread.

TWEED IS A WOVEN FABRIC AND SO TENDS TO FRAY MORE THAN NON-WOVEN FELT. HANDLE THE CUT-OUT SHAPES CAREFULLY, ESPECIALLY WHEN REMOVING THE BACKING PAPER.

Floral Drawstring Bag

Cath Kidston

SKILL RATING: 1
WHAT YOU WILL NEED...

- Drawstring bag
- Bondaweb
- Cotton fabric print: 25cm square
- Iron
- Sewing thread to match fabric
- Sewing workbox (see page 15)

Simple bags like this have endless uses, especially when travelling. Why not make one to protect your favourite shoes?

1 The reversed outline motifs for this project can be found on the Flowers template card. To fit my bag, which is 28cm x 31cm, I increased the size to 120% and used 17 flowers: create your own look by making the blooms smaller or larger.

2 Iron Bondaweb onto the wrong side of the cotton fabric, then cut each flower out around the inner and outer lines.

3 Peel away the backing papers and lay the flowers across the front of the bag. Shuffle them about until you have a pleasing arrangement – you may need to add a couple extra or take one or two away. Fuse the flowers in place with a warm iron.

4 To secure the edges, work a round of short straight stitches around each flower (see page 20), using matching sewing thread.

APPLIQUÉ IS A WONDERFUL WAY TO RECYCLE FORGOTTEN FABRICS: HERE I USED A REMNANT OF VINTAGE FLORAL DRESS PRINT TO ADD COLOUR AND PATTERN TO A PLAIN BAG.

Clothing

There is nothing more pleasing than recycling an old piece of clothing to give it a whole new lease on life. A good trick is to dye it first – perhaps start with an old white T-shirt than has gone a bit grey. It's great fun seeing it transformed in the dye bucket. Then add a finishing touch of appliqué!

College Jumper

IF YOU BELONG TO A CLUB OR TEAM, YOU COULD HAVE A GO AT CREATING A MATCHING SET OF THESE FOR ALL ITS MEMBERS.

You can transform an ordinary V-neck into a vintage-style college jumper, simply by stitching on elbow patches and felt letters.

1 Choose your initials from the outline on the Alphabet template card, enlarge as necessary, and trace onto Bondaweb. Cut the letters out roughly.

2 Place the letters, adhesive-side down, on the felt. Lay a pressing cloth over the top, then fuse them in place with a warm iron. Cut out accurately.

3 Peel away the backing paper from each letter. Place the jumper on your ironing board and position the letters, right side up, to the right of the neckline. Iron them in place, again using a pressing cloth.

4 Using red embroidery thread, work a round of straight stitches (see page 20) around the edge of each letter to secure the felt and to add extra decoration.

Cath Kidston

SKILL RATING: 1
WHAT YOU WILL NEED...

• Finely knit turquoise jumper
• Bondaweb
• Iron and pressing cloth
• Felt: 6cm x 12cm pink
• Embroidery thread in red and pink
• Sheet of paper
• Cotton fabric print: 15cm x 20cm
• Sewing workbox (see page 15)

5 To make the template for the patches, cut an 8cm by 15cm rectangle of paper. Fold it in quarters, then draw a curve across the unfolded corners. Cut along this line, through all the layers, then open out the paper.

6 Draw around the outline of the template twice, on the paper side of the Bondaweb. Iron the adhesive side to the wrong side of the printed fabric, then cut out the patches along the pencil lines.

7 Remembering your pressing cloth, iron the patches to the back of the sleeves, making sure they are both at the same level. Embellish the edges with blanket stitch (see page 21), using pink embroidery thread.

ABCDE

TO POSITION THE PATCHES, TURN THE EDGE OF THE CUFF UP TO THE SHOULDER LINE, THEN PLACE THE CENTRE OF THE PATCH ALONG THE FOLD.

Cowboy
Skirt

IF YOU LIKE, YOU CAN APPLIQUÉ ALL THE WAY AROUND THE HEM (YOU'LL NEED TO ALLOW MORE FELT FOR THIS) OR JUST SEW A FEW MOTIFS TO THE FRONT OF YOUR SKIRT.

Cath Kidston

SKILL RATING: 3
WHAT YOU WILL NEED...

- Red skirt
- Bondaweb, iron and pressing cloth
- Felt: 25cm square each of light stone, warm brown, light green and dark green; 10cm square each of peat brown, dark stone and red
- Woven fabric: scraps of blue gingham, denim and red tweed
- Sewing thread to match fabrics
- Embroidery thread in brown, dark blue, light blue and green
- Dressmaker's fading-ink pen
- Sewing workbox (see page 15)

Even if you're not off to a Rodeo, hoedown or line dancing session, this swingy skirt will put a spring in your step!

1 Enlarge the reversed outlines on the Cowboy template card by 115%. Trace around the cowboy and horse onto Bondaweb, cut out roughly and fuse onto light stone felt. Cut out accurately, peel off the paper and iron onto the skirt, 15cm from the hem and a little off to the side. Make sure you always use a pressing cloth when you're working with felt.

2 Now build up the details, starting with gingham shirt and denim jeans. The cowboy's hair, the horse's mane, bridle and hooves are peat brown felt and the shadows on its body, the saddle and the hat dark stone.

3 Use warm brown felt for the main holster, saddle strap and the boot, and red tweed for the holster detail and the neckerchief. Straight stitch (see page 20) around each piece in matching sewing thread, then work the facial details in brown embroidery thread.

4 Draw the dust cloud and the lasso with a fading-ink pen and chain stitch (see page 21) over the lines: dark blue for the lasso and light blue for the cloud.

5 Add a cactus on either side of the cowboy, using two shades of green felt. Chain stitch the grass with dark green embroidery thread.

6 Decorate the back of the skirt with two more cactuses, and a wagon cut from warm brown felt with details in red and light stone.

CHOOSE A FULL, GATHERED SKIRT IN A HEAVY COTTON WEAVE FOR THAT AUTHENTIC COWGIRL LOOK.

Songbird Slippers

THE FLYING SONGBIRDS
THAT APPEAR ON THE
TEMPLATE CARD WITH THIS
MOTIF WOULD BE A GOOD
ALTERNATIVE DESIGN. YOU
COULD EVEN SWAP THE
COLOURS AROUND TO MAKE
THEM INTO BLUEBIRDS.

Cath Kidston

SKILL RATING: 2
WHAT YOU WILL NEED...

• Pair of plain slippers
• Bondaweb
• Iron and pressing cloth
• Felt: 10cm x 15cm light stone;
scraps of red, dark brown, pink
  and white
• Sewing thread to match felts
• Embroidery thread in dark brown
• Sewing workbox (see page 15)

Pad about the house to your heart's content in these customised slippers.

1 You'll find the reversed outline of the songbird motif on the Songbird template card. I enlarged it by 200%, to 7cm tall to fit these grey jersey slippers, but you may wish to make it slightly larger or smaller.

2 Trace around the complete bird outline onto Bondaweb. Cut out roughly, fuse (using a pressing cloth) onto light stone felt and snip around the pencil line.

3 Now cut out the red breast, brown beak, and the pink and white head details. Peel the papers off these four pieces and carefully iron them in place on the main bird shape, again with a pressing cloth. Remove the backing from the bird and pin it to the centre front of the left slipper.

4 Work a round of straight stitches around each piece (see page 20), using matching sewing thread. Add a tiny brown felt shape for the foot and work a few stitches in dark brown embroidery thread for the eye.

5 Decorate the right slipper in the same way, reversing the template so that the two birds are facing each other.

IF PINNING THE FELT TO THE SLIPPER FABRIC PROVES A LITTLE TRICKY, TRY USING A DAB OF ADHESIVE FROM A GLUE STICK TO KEEP IT IN PLACE AS YOU SEW.

Racing
Driver Scarf

Cath Kidston

SKILL RATING: 2
WHAT YOU WILL NEED...

- Strawberry pink scarf
- Bondaweb
- Iron and pressing cloth
- Lightweight tweed: 20cm x 20cm square of brown; 10cm square of red
- Felt: scraps of beige, pale beige and dark brown
- Dressmaker's fading-ink pen
- Sewing thread to match fabrics
- Embroidery thread in brown
- 4 brown buttons, for the wheels
- Sewing workbox (see page 15)

Wait for the chequered flag to go down...

1 Trace all the elements that make up the top racing car outline on the Racing Car template card onto Bondaweb. Draw the driver's head and shoulders in a single piece following the dotted line, then his helmet and jacket separately. Cut out the pieces, 5mm from the outlines.

2 Iron the adhesive side of the two car parts onto the brown tweed and cut around the edge. Remember to snip the small slit across the bonnet.

3 Now cut the helmet, jacket and wheels from red tweed and make the side vent, hubcaps and oval from beige felt. The driver is in pale beige felt and his goggles, the steering wheel and seat back are brown felt. Remember to use a pressing cloth whenever you are ironing felt.

4 Remove the backing papers. Centre the two parts of the car at one end of the scarf, 13cm from the hem. Iron in place, then add the wheels and hubcaps. Fuse the driver in position and add his goggles, helmet and jacket. Finish with his seatback, vent and the oval.

5 Edge each of the shapes with a round of straight stitches (see page 20), using matching sewing thread.

6 Draw a number onto the oval with a fading-ink pen and straight stitch over it, using brown embroidery thread. Finish off by sewing a button to the centre of each hubcap.

7 Decorate the other end of the scarf in the same way with the second racing car. Reverse the outline so that it is going in the opposite direction.

IF YOU FIND THE BROWN FELT DETAILS A BIT TOO FIDDLY, YOU COULD EMBROIDER THEM IN SATIN STITCH INSTEAD (SEE PAGE 20).

Starry
T-shirt

IF YOU PREFER A MORE FLOWERY LOOK, CHOOSE A PRINTED FABRIC TO MAKE YOUR STARS.

Cath Kidston

SKILL RATING: 1
WHAT YOU WILL NEED...

- Laundered cotton T-shirt
- Bondaweb
- Iron
- Woven cotton fabric: scraps of plain colours, washed and pressed
- Thread plait or assorted reels of sewing thread
- Sewing workbox (see page 15)

Give yourself maximum star rating with a shooting star T-shirt.

1 Turn to the star outlines on the Stars template card, and trace 60 stars in different sizes onto the paper side of your Bondaweb. Cut each one out roughly.

2 Gather together your fabric pieces and iron the adhesive side of the stars onto a selection of your favourite colours. Cut them all out, following the pencil line precisely.

3 Lay the top of the T-shirt across your ironing board and arrange the stars over the sleeves and around the neckline, reserving about 16 for the back of the sleeves. Move them around until you have a good balance of size and colour across the design.

4 Iron the stars in place, one at a time, starting at the bottom edge of the arrangement. Peel the backing paper off each one in turn and press them with the tip of the iron. Decorate the back of the sleeves in the same way.

5 Add even more colour to the twinkling stars by securing them with contrasting sewing thread. Sew a round of short straight stitches around each star, working the stitches at right angles to the stars (see page 20).

THE MORE FABRICS YOU HAVE, THE MORE EFFECTIVE THIS DESIGN WILL BE, BUT KEEP THEM ALL WITHIN THE SAME TONAL RANGE.

Spotty
Beret

Cath Kidston

SKILL RATING: 1
WHAT YOU WILL NEED...

• Red beret
• Bondaweb
• Iron and pressing cloth
• Felt: 15cm x 30cm white
• Embroidery thread in white
• Sewing workbox (see page 15)

Bring out your inner pixie with this fun spotty toadstool beret.

1 Trace the largest outline spot on the Bubbles template card onto the paper side of the Bondaweb 14 times. Cut each circle out roughly, about 5mm from the edge.

2 Fuse the adhesive side of the spots onto the white felt, placing the cloth over the fabric first, so that the heat of the iron won't distort the felt. Carefully cut out each one, following the pencil line closely.

3 Peel the backing papers off the spots. Spacing them evenly, arrange five of them around the beret's stalk. Press them in place with a warm iron, again using a protective cloth.

4 Arrange the remaining spots in a second ring, just outside the first. Iron them in place as before.

5 Secure each spot in place with a circle of straight stitches (see page 20), using white embroidery thread. Sew with a large-eyed needle that will pass easily through the thick wool fabric.

YOU DON'T HAVE TO USE THE SPOTS, OF COURSE. MAYBE YOU'D PREFER STARS, FLOWERS OR EVEN TINY DOG-BONE SHAPES!

Boat
T-shirt

A DARK NAVY T-SHIRT WOULD GIVE THIS MOTIF A BOLDER, MORE DRAMATIC IMPACT.

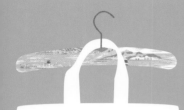

Cath Kidston

SKILL RATING: 3
WHAT YOU WILL NEED...

- Laundered cotton T-shirt
- Bondaweb
- Iron and pressing cloth
- Felt: 10cm x 25cm white; 6cm x 25cm blue; 10cm square of red; 3cm x 10cm yellow; scraps of green and brown
- Sewing thread to match felts
- Dressmaker's fading-ink pen
- Embroidery thread in blue, brown and red
- Sewing workbox (see page 15)

Prepare for a life on the open waves with this jaunty, nautical T-shirt, perfect for a seaside holiday.

1 Start by tracing the cloud outline on the Sailing-boat template card onto the paper side of the Bondaweb. Cut out roughly and iron the adhesive to white felt. Always use a pressing cloth to protect the felt. Cut along the outline, remove the paper, and iron the felt onto the T-shirt. Using white thread, sew short straight stitches all around the edge of the cloud (see page 20).

2 Trace all the waves onto Bondaweb, cut out roughly around the outside edge, then fuse onto the blue felt. Cut out the long top wave, peel off the backing and iron it on just below the horizon. Add the other waves, one at a time, and secure with blue thread.

3 Next, cut out the red and the yellow felt sails. Iron them in position and add the white stripes. Stitch in place with straight stitches, using matching sewing thread.

4 Cut out and iron on the three tiny pennants for the small boats, then finish off with the four hulls in the appropriate coloured felt. Secure with straight stitches, using matching sewing thread.

5 The details are worked with embroidery thread. Sew blue chain stitch (see page 21) around the top edge of the clouds, working on the T-shirt, along the blue outline shown in the coloured template.

6 Using a fading-ink pen, draw in the other details – the masts, the seagulls and the pennant on the large boat. Using embroidery thread, work straight stitches over these lines: brown for the masts and seagulls, and red for the pennant.

DON'T FORGET TO USE A PRESSING CLOTH WHEN YOU'RE WORKING WITH FELT OR IT WILL BECOME DISTORTED AND LOSE ITS SHAPE!

Kids

An item like this beautiful appliquéd blanket will become a treasured heirloom. If you don't have the patience to make such a large piece, try the technique on a small bag or sweatshirt. With an older sister, I had endless hand-me-downs and I wish my mother had given my clothes such exciting updates!

Floral
Frock

Cath Kidston

SKILL RATING: 3
WHAT YOU WILL NEED...

- Simple tunic dress
- Lightweight non-woven iron-on interfacing
- Dressmaker's fading-ink pen
- Iron and pressing cloth
- Embroidery thread in purple, light orange, brown, stone, pink, red, green and turquoise
- Sewing workbox (see page 15)

This adorable frock has a timeless charm, which will guarantee that any little girl who wears it gets off to a head start in the fashion stakes.

1 The floral embroidery is deceptively simple to work. Read the detailed instructions on pages 22–3 to find out how it is done, then turn to the outline of the Circus Flowers template card.

2 Using a fading-ink pen, trace two large and six small flower outlines onto the smooth side of the iron-on interfacing, ignoring the dotted lines. You will also need eight large and four small leaves. Cut all the motifs out around the outside edge.

3 Arrange the shapes in the corners of the yoke of the dress, either following the photograph on the left or adapting the design to suit your particular dress. Iron them in place, using a pressing cloth.

4 Embroider all the flowers in satin stitch (see page 20). Fill in each area of each shape with a block of stitches following the colours used on the opposite page, and angling the stitches towards the centre of the flowers.

TINY DETAILS ADD CHARACTER: NOTE HOW THE BUTTONHOLES
ARE OUTLINED WITH GREEN THREAD AND QUIRKY REPLACEMENT
BUTTONS COMPLEMENT THE EMBROIDERY.

Cowboy
Denim Jacket

Be part of your own Wild
West adventure with a
customised cowboy
jacket. Yee-ha!

Cath Kidston

**SKILL RATING: 3
WHAT YOU WILL NEED...**

- Denim jacket
- Bondaweb
- Iron and pressing cloth
- Felt: 20cm square of light stone;
  10cm square each of red, blue,
  dark stone, brown, light green
  and dark green
- Embroidery thread to match felts
- Chalk pencil
- Sewing workbox (see page 15)

1 Trace the cowboy and horse outlines on the Cowboy
template card onto Bondaweb. Cut out roughly, iron onto
light stone felt, then cut along the pencil line. Take off the
backing and iron the motif to the centre of the back of the
jacket. Always use a pressing cloth when working with felt.

2 Make the cowboy's shirt from red felt and his leg from
blue as above, then fuse them onto the main motif.

3 The next layer is of dark stone felt: use this for the
shadows on the horse, the saddle, scarf and hat. The
boot, hooves, mane, bridle, pistol and strap details are
in brown felt. Finally make the holster from red felt.

4 Secure each piece of the finished appliqué with a round
of short straight stitches, worked at right angles to the
edge (see page 20). Use all six strands of the stranded
embroidery thread and match the colours to the felt.

5 With brown thread, embroider straight-stitch details onto the cowboy's hat and hair. Work
two tiny stitches for his eyes, and pairs of stitches for the horse's eye and nostril. Outline the
saddle in backstitch.

6 With a chalk pencil, draw in the dust cloud, grass and lasso. Embroider over the lines,
using blue backstitch for the cloud, green straight stitch for the grass and light stone-
coloured chain stitch for the lasso (see page 21).

7 For the cactus on the pocket, make the main shape from light green felt and the shadow
from dark green. Edge both layers with matching straight stitches as before, then embroider
the flowers in red and the grass in green.

THIS JACKET FITS A TODDLER: IF YOU ARE MAKING IT FOR AN
OLDER CHILD YOU SHOULD ENLARGE THE TEMPLATE SO THAT IT
FILLS THE WHOLE OF BACK PANEL.

Racing Card Sweatshirt

IF YOU ARE MAKING THIS TOP AS A BIRTHDAY GIFT, YOU COULD CHANGE THE NUMBER EMBROIDERED ON THE FELT OVAL TO THE CHILD'S AGE.

Cath Kidston

SKILL RATING: 2
WHAT YOU WILL NEED...

- Grey cotton sweatshirt
- Bondaweb
- Iron and pressing cloth
- Felt: 20cm x 10cm green; 15cm square of red; 10cm square each of brown and dark stone
- Sewing thread to match felts
- Embroidery thread in light stone, brown and blue
- Dressmaker's fading-ink pen
- Sewing workbox (see page 15)

Make this for the boy racer in your life – even if his favourite vehicle is still only a tricycle!

1 Turn to the reversed outlines on the Racing Car template card. Trace all the parts that make up the driver and his car, the two trees, the hedge, grass and fence onto Bondaweb, then add an extra tree. Cut the pieces out roughly.

2 Iron the Bondaweb to the various felts: the car, jacket, helmet and fence onto red; the wheels, seat, steering wheel, goggles and trunks to brown; the oval, vent and hubcaps to stone; the trees, hedge and tuft of grass to green. Always use a pressing cloth when working with felt. Cut out the motifs accurately, and remove the paper backings as you need the pieces.

3 Spread the sweatshirt out on your ironing board. Position the car across the chest. Tuck a tree trunk under the boot and fuse in place.

4 Add the wheels and driver, then fuse on his helmet, goggles and jacket, the steering wheel and seatback, the vent, the oval and finally, the hubcaps.

5 Finish off by arranging the countryside motifs on either side as shown: two trees and the grass to the right; the hedge, fence and third tree to the left. Tuck the trunks under the trees and place the fence over the hedge.

6 Anchor each felt shape with short straight stitches (see page 20), using matching sewing thread. Lastly, draw on the details with fading-ink pen and work with embroidery thread: light stone and brown backstitch (see page 21) on the wheels and for the number, blue straight stitch on the vent and light stone satin stitch (see page 20) for the windscreen.

THE TREES AND OTHER COUNTRYSIDE MOTIFS HAVE BEEN REARRANGED TO SUIT THIS DESIGN. LAY THEM OUT FIRST TO CHECK THE SPACING AND HOW THE FINAL DESIGN WILL LOOK.

Antique Cardigan

WHY NOT CHANGE THE BUTTONS
ON THE CARDIGAN TO MATCH
THE COLOURS OF THE
EMBROIDERY THREADS?

Cath Kidston

SKILL RATING: 3
WHAT YOU WILL NEED...

- Finely knit cream V-neck cardigan
- Lightweight non-woven iron-on interfacing
- Dressmaker's fading-ink pen
- Iron and pressing cloth
- Embroidery thread in pink, red, antique white and green
- Sewing workbox (see page 15)

Turn a plain garment into a keepsake to hand down through the generations.

1 Photocopy the flower outlines on the Circus Flowers template card, increasing the size to 115%. Make a second enlarged copy, which is a mirror image of the first. Trace one large and three small roses, plus three buds, from each sheet onto the smooth (non-adhesive) side of the iron-on interfacing, using a fading-ink pen.

2 Cut out all the flowers and arrange them symmetrically on either side of the neckline. Fuse in place using an iron and a pressing cloth to protect the cardigan.

3 You'll find detailed instructions on how to embroider over lightweight non-woven iron-on interfacing on page 23. Read through these, then fill in the rose and bud outlines with pink, red and antique white satin stitch (see page 20). Add a few green stitches to the centre of each rose.

4 Embroider the leaves in satin stitch, angling the stitches towards the centre vein and finish off by working the stems in backstitch (see page 21).

THIS IS A PROJECT FOR AN EXPERIENCED MAKER, BUT IF YOU ARE A BEGINNER, INCREASE THE SIZE OF THE ROSES BY 200% AND EMBROIDER THEM ON A LARGE SCALE.

Alphabet
Cushion

IF YOU HAVEN'T THE TIME
TO STITCH THE ENTIRE
ALPHABET, WORK JUST A
TWO-LETTER MONOGRAM IN
THE CENTRE OF THE COVER.

Cath Kidston

SKILL RATING: 3
WHAT YOU WILL NEED...

- 45cm cream cushion cover
- Bondaweb
- Iron and pressing cloth
- Felt: 10cm x 30cm each of
  pale pink, dark pink, mid blue,
  light blue, green, yellow and
  brown
- Old newspapers and tea towel
- Dressmaker's fading-ink pen
- Embroidery thread to match felts
- Sewing workbox (see page 15)

Nearly as easy to make as ABC, this cushion would
be a wonderful nursery accessory.

1 Enlarge the reversed letter outlines on the Alphabet
template card by 250% so that they are 7.5cm tall. Trace
all of them except D, H, S, U and V onto the paper side
of the Bondaweb and cut out 5mm from the edge.

2 Iron the letters onto the various felt pieces, then cut
out neatly. Always use a pressing cloth when working
with felt. Cut the remaining letters from the photocopy
and turn them the right side up.

3 Spread the newspapers on your work surface with the
tea towel on top to make an impromptu ironing board.
Lay the cushion cover over the tea towel.

4 Peel the paper from the felt letters and position both
these and the paper cutouts across the cover, referring to
the picture opposite as a placement guide. Pin the paper
letters in place and iron the felt letters in place, using a
pressing cloth.

5 Draw around each paper letter with a fading-ink pen
and then unpin them. Embroider over these outlines in chain stitch (see page 21). Work a
round of contrasting blanket stitch around each felt letter (see page 21).

USE THE FINISHED PHOTOGRAPH AS YOUR GUIDE TO CHOOSING
COLOURS FOR THE FELT LETTERS AND THEIR EMBROIDERED
EDGINGS, OR CHOOSE YOUR OWN COLOUR SCHEME.

Starry
Bib

FOLLOWING NURSERY TRADITION,
YOU COULD MAKE A BIB WITH
JUST PINK STARS FOR A GIRL OR
ALL BLUE FOR A BOY.

Cath Kidston

SKILL RATING: 1
WHAT YOU WILL NEED...

- White towelling bib
- Bondaweb
- Iron
- Plain cotton fabric: 10cm square each of green, pink, yellow and blue
- Sewing thread to match fabrics
- Sewing workbox (see page 15)

This shooting star bib will bring a touch of sophistication to the messiest lunchtime!

1 The outline star templates are on the Stars template card. Use a sharp pencil to trace them onto the paper side of the Bondaweb, then add three more so that you have 22 in all. Cut all of the stars out roughly.

2 Following the manufacturer's instructions, iron five or six stars onto each of the cotton fabrics. Trim them neatly around the pencil lines.

3 Lay the bib out flat on your ironing board. Peel the backing papers from the stars and arrange them on the bib using the photograph opposite as a guide. Fuse them in place with a cool iron.

4 Anchor the stars with straight stitching around the edge of each one (see page 20), using matching sewing thread.

BABIES HAVE NO RESPECT FOR THEIR BEST OUTFITS, SO THE BIB WILL INEVITABLY NEED FREQUENT WASHING. SOAK IT IN GENTLE STAIN REMOVER AS NECESSARY, AND LAUNDER ON A COOL CYCLE.

Tiny Tote

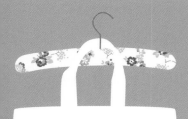

Cath Kidston

SKILL RATING: 2
WHAT YOU WILL NEED...

- Small tweed tote bag
- Bondaweb
- Iron and pressing cloth
- Cotton fabric: 15cm x 20cm red
polka dot; 10cm x 15cm green
polka dot; 10cm x 25cm floral
- Felt: scrap of brown
- Sewing thread to match fabrics
- Sewing workbox (see page 15)

Little girls love to keep their treasures in a special bag, so these little totes are guaranteed to delight.

1 Enlarge the outline of the flower basket motif on the Basket of Flowers template card to fit your bag's proportions: I increased the size by 230% for my 24cm-square tote.

2 Using a sharp pencil, trace the basket, handle, leaves, flowers and their centres onto the paper side of the Bondaweb. Cut the shapes out roughly.

3 Iron the Bondaweb pieces onto the wrong side of the fabrics: the basket and handle go on the red polka dot cotton; the leaves on the green dots and the flowers on the floral print. Fuse the flower centres to the felt, using a pressing cloth.

4 Cut out all the shapes and carefully remove the backing papers. Position the basket near the bottom of your bag, then place the handle a short distance above it.

5 Arrange the three flowers so that they overlap the areas indicated by the dotted lines. Put the leaves in place, tucking them under the flowers where shown and finally add the flower centres. Iron the completed design onto the bag, remembering your pressing cloth to protect the background.

6 Referring to the diagram on page 165, sew each appliqué shape to the bag with a round of straight stitches (see page 20), using matching sewing thread.

THIS FOLK-ART STYLE MOTIF WOULD WORK EQUALLY WELL ON THE FRONT OF A T-SHIRT OR PERHAPS ON A COTTON APRON FOR BUDDING CHEFS.

Racing Car
Blanket

Cath Kidston

SKILL RATING: 2
WHAT YOU WILL NEED...

- Blue single blanket
- Bondaweb
- Iron and pressing cloth
- Felt: small amount each of red, stone, brown, green and blue
- Sewing thread to match the felt
- Embroidery thread in stone, brown and blue
- Sewing workbox (see page 15)

The procession of vintage cars along the border of this cosy blanket will inspire endless bedtime tales of record-breaking racers.

1 The racing car motifs are on the Racing Car template card you'll see that the outline versions are both travelling in the same direction. With a pencil, trace all the elements of the top car onto Bondaweb and cut them out roughly.

2 Start with the red car. Iron the Bondaweb onto felt: red for the car, helmet and jacket; brown for the wheels, steering wheel and goggles; stone for the driver, oval, windscreen, vent and hubcaps. Use a pressing cloth when working with felt. Trim carefully around each pencil line.

3 Peel away the backings and iron the two parts of the car centrally onto the blanket, 2cm from the satin binding. Add the driver, then his jacket, goggles and helmet. Fuse on the other elements.

4 Secure every shape with straight stitches (see page 20), using matching sewing thread. The details are embroidered on with embroidery thread: stone and brown backstitch (see page 21) for the wheels and number, with blue straight stitch on the vent.

5 Now appliqué a blue car on each side of the first, leaving 8–10cm between them. The detail on the bonnet is different for these cars and they do not have a vent – otherwise the method is just the same. Finally, add two more red cars towards the corners, with a similar gap between them.

6 Fill in the spaces between the cars with a trees, bushes, fences and tufts of grass. Refer to the photograph opposite to see how to arrange these.

FIVE CARS FIT NEATLY ACROSS A SINGLE BLANKET 150CM WIDE.
MEASURE YOURS FIRST TO WORK OUT HOW MANY MOTIFS
YOU'LL NEED AND HOW MUCH SPACE TO LEAVE BETWEEN THEM.

Gifts

There is nothing more touching than a home-made gift that has had care and thought put into it. Here are some ideas for things to make, and many are very quick – it's usually just a case of thinking ahead!

Framed Sailing-boats

IF YOU LIKE THE LOOK OF THIS PICTURE, WHY NOT USE ONE OF THE OTHER DESIGNS IN THE SAME WAY — THE COTTAGE, PERHAPS, OR THE SONGBIRDS?

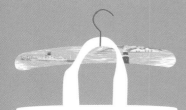

Cath Kidston

SKILL RATING: 3
WHAT YOU WILL NEED...

- Old picture frame
- Linen: piece 3cm larger all around than the frame's opening
- Bondaweb
- Iron and pressing cloth
- Felt: 10cm x 25cm white; 20cm x 25cm blue; 20cm square of red; 5cm x 15cm yellow; scraps of green and brown
- Embroidery thread to match felts
- Dressmaker's fading-ink pen
- Sewing workbox (see page 15)

A nautical theme works anywhere in the house: these sailing-boats would look equally at home in a kitchen, bedroom or living space.

1 Enlarge the reversed sailing-boat outline on the Sailing-boat template card to fit within your frame. Make a couple of copies at different sizes and choose the one that you like best.

2 Start by tracing the waves onto Bondaweb. Iron them onto blue felt and cut out. Always use a pressing cloth when working with felt. Peel the paper from the top wave and position it so that the horizon lies two-thirds of the way down the frame. Now add the other waves.

3 Next, cut the sails from red and yellow felt. Iron them in position and add the white stripes and red pennants. Finish off by making the hulls from the appropriate colour felt.

4 Stitch around each shape with straight stitches (see page 20), using matching embroidery thread. For the smaller sails, stitch right across each narrow white stripe, rather than sewing along each side.

5 Embroider the remaining details. Draw the cloud line (you'll see how far this extends on the coloured template) with a fading-ink pen and stitch over it in blue chain stitch (see page 21). Work the seagulls, masts and ropes in brown straight stitches.

THE SCRUFFIEST PICTURE FRAME CAN BE ENLIVENED WITH FRESH PAINT. SAND IT DOWN LIGHTLY, THEN BUY A SMALL SAMPLE POT OF PAINT AND APPLY TWO OR THREE COATS TO CONCEAL THE OLD FINISH.

Dog Cushion

IF YOUR DOG IS A FLUFFY
FEMALE, YOU MAY PREFER
TO CHANGE THE BOWL TO
A SPOTTY PINK BOWL
VARIATION TO SUIT HER
CHARACTER.

Cath Kidston

SKILL RATING: 1
WHAT YOU WILL NEED...

- Dog bed
- Bondaweb
- Iron and pressing cloth
- Felt: 15cm x 25cm each of brown
  and turquoise; 10cm x 15cm
  white; 20cm square of red
- Linen: 10cm x 25cm off-white
- Sewing thread to match fabrics
- Sewing workbox (see page 15)

Don't forget the family pet when it comes to giving presents. Every dog's favourite items – a ball, a bowl and a bone – feature on this comfortable cushion.

1 Enlarge the three accessory outlines on the Stanley template card by 300% so that they are on the right scale for the bed.

2 Trace the bowl, the oval detail and the 13 spots onto the paper side of your Bondaweb. Cut out and iron onto felt: turquoise for the bowl, brown for the oval detail and white for the dots. Remember your pressing cloth. Cut out the motifs accurately.

3 Peel the backings from the oval and the dots, then fuse them to the bowl, following the coloured motif on the Stanley template card for the positions.

4 Remove the paper from the bowl and secure the dots and oval with short straight stitches (see page 20), using matching sewing thread. Pin the bowl across one corner of the cushion and straight stitch in place.

5 Cut the bone from linen and its shadow details from brown felt. Take the paper off the shadows and iron them to the bone. Now remove the paper from the bone, pin it to the cushion to the right of the bowl and secure with cream sewing thread.

6 Make the ball in red felt with brown curve details. Peel the backings off the curves and fuse them to the ball. Take the paper off the ball and staight stitch along the curves with brown thread. Add the ball to the cushion, to the left of the bowl.

USE A DOUBLE LENGTH OF THREAD TO STITCH THE MOTIFS TO
THE BED: YOU WILL NEED THE EXTRA STRENGTH (AND MAYBE A
THIMBLE) WHEN YOU ARE SEWING THROUGH THE THICK FABRIC.

Cath Kidston

SKILL RATING: 1
WHAT YOU WILL NEED...

- Selection of greetings-card blanks or sheets of lightweight cardboard
- Bondaweb
- Iron and pressing cloth
- Fabric: selection of scraps
- Glue stick
- Tracing paper
- Assortment of paper in different patterns and textures

A handmade card means far more than any shop-bought greeting: show your family and friends you care by creating a one-off original.

1 To make a fabric design, trace the reversed motifs onto Bondaweb, iron them onto the back of your cloth and cut out as for fabric appliqué. If you are using felt, use a pressing cloth.

2 Remove the backing papers and fix the motifs to the card with a glue stick (the heat of an iron would damage the card).

3 To make a paper design, like this colourful flowerpot, use an old-fashioned tracing technique. Draw the reversed outline onto tracing paper. Turn the paper over and rub your pencil, slightly flattened, over the lines.

4 Transfer each shape onto the wrong side of the decorative paper by drawing over the original pencil line once again. Find out the order of assembly for the multi-layered designs by turning to the appliqué instructions on pages 18–19: the flowerpot is on the Flowerpot template card.

BECOME A MAGPIE AND COLLECT PRETTY POSTCARDS, DIAMANTÉS, SILVER FOIL, WRAPPING PAPER, SWEET PACKETS, ODD BUTTONS, RIBBONS AND OTHER SCRAP MATERIALS TO RECYCLE INTO CARDS.

Stanley
Cushion

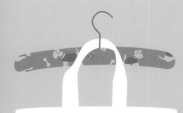

Cath Kidston

SKILL RATING: 3
WHAT YOU WILL NEED...

- Cushion cover and pad
- Tracing paper
- Soft leather or suede:
  10cm x 12cm dark brown;
  25cm square of light brown;
  scrap of red
- Glue stick
- Embroidery thread in dark
  brown, red and light brown
- Leather needle
- Dressmaker's fading-ink pen
- Sewing workbox (see page 15)

Who could fail to be delighted with this endearing Stanley cushion cover?

1 With a sharp pencil, draw the Stanley outline on the Stanley template card onto tracing paper. Cut out the shapes to make your pattern pieces.

2 Draw around the patterns onto the wrong side of the leather, using the pencil (or a white crayon if it's very dark). Cut the collar from red, the back and right leg markings from dark brown and the other pieces from light brown. Turn them all right side up.

3 Referring back to the template, draw Stanley's features on the head. Using a leather needle, embroider them in dark brown thread, using small straight stitches (see page 20) to build up the ears, eyes and nose, and backstitch (see page 21) for the mouth.

4 Remove the pad from the cushion and reassemble the image on the centre front. Fit the pieces together like a jigsaw but leave 2–3mm between them. Attach each one to the cover with a thin layer of adhesive from a glue stick. Place a large book on the cover, to weight the pieces down, and leave until the glue is dry.

5 Again using the leather needle, secure the leather pieces with straight stitches, using matching embroidery thread. Put the pad back in the cover.

THIS CUSHION HAS IMPECCABLE ECO-CREDENTIALS: THE LIGHT
BROWN LEATHER WAS SALVAGED FROM AN OLD JACKET AND THE
DARK BROWN SCRAPS CAME FROM AN OUTWORN BAG.

Felt-Leaved Needle Book

AS A VARIATION ON THIS
THEME, YOU COULD CUT
SEVERAL RECTANGLES OF
PAPER AND STITCH THEM
INSIDE THE FELT COVER TO
MAKE A SPECIAL NOTEBOOK.

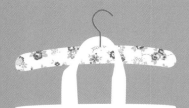

SKILL RATING: 2
WHAT YOU WILL NEED...

- Bondaweb
- Iron and pressing cloth
- Felt: 12cm x 19cm pink;
  8cm x 10cm blue; 10cm x 24cm
  yellow; scraps of red, pink,
  yellow and green, for the appliqué
- Sewing thread to match felts
- Embroidery thread in blue, yellow
  and green
- 3 buttons
- Sewing workbox (see page 15)

This pretty needle case would make a welcome present for the keen stitchers amongst your family and friends – if you can bring yourself to part with it!

1 Using the outlines on the Circus Flowers template card, trace the three layers of a big flower, two small flowers, four leaves and two dots onto Bondaweb. Cut them out roughly and iron onto the felt scraps, matching the colours opposite. Always remember a pressing cloth when working with felt.

2 Cut each shape around the pencil line. Peel off the papers and arrange the red flower, pink flowers, dots and leaves in the bottom left corner of the blue felt. Iron in place, then add the pink and yellow layers to the red flower.

3 Now add some embellishment. Work straight stitches (see page 20) around each layer of the red flower, the pink flowers and the dots, using matching sewing thread. Sew a single straight stitch on each leaf in green embroidery thread. Stitch a button to the centre of each flower.

4 To make up the book, place the yellow felt centrally on the pink felt and fold in half lengthways to make a pink book with yellow pages. Pin the two pieces together, close to the fold.

5 Stitch along the left side of the book, by hand or machine. Pin the blue felt to the front cover, aligning the left edge with the stitching. Straight stitch it in place with tiny – almost invisible – stitches, using blue thread.

6 As a final touch, work a line of blue stitches around three sides of the pink felt and yellow stitches around the blue felt, using embroidery thread.

THREAD SOME OF YOUR NEEDLES WITH LENGTHS OF DIFFERENT
COLOURED THREADS AND KEEP THEM TO HAND IN YOUR BOOK.
THIS WILL SAVE TIME IF YOU NEED TO DO AN INSTANT REPAIR.

Flannel &
Towel Set

IF YOU'RE MAKING THIS FOR YOURSELF, WHY NOT CONTINUE THE THEME AND APPLIQUÉ FLOWERS ONTO THE BATH MAT AND EVEN YOUR DRESSING GOWN?

Cath Kidston

SKILL RATING: 1
WHAT YOU WILL NEED...

- White flannel and hand-towel
- Two 9cm wide strips of white cotton fabric: one 8cm longer than the face cloth and the other 8cm longer than the towel's width
- Bondaweb
- Iron
- Plain cotton fabric: small amount each of light blue, green and pink
- Sewing thread to match fabrics
- Sewing workbox (see page 15)

This bathroom set is a luxurious accompaniment to a long, pampering soak, complete with scented soap and fragrant essential oils.

1 The flower motif is on the Breakfast template card. Enlarge it by 280% to about 3cm, then trace it onto the paper side of the Bondaweb. You will need six flowers for a 25cm square face cloth and 12 for a 50cm wide hand towel – trace more for a larger towel.

2 Cut the flowers out roughly and iron the adhesive side onto the light blue, green and pink cotton fabrics, making sure you have an equal number of each colour. Trim them neatly around the edge and snip out the centre holes with short-bladed scissors. Peel off the papers.

3 Leaving a 5cm space at each end, arrange six flowers along the centre of the short fabric strip in a pink-blue-green colour sequence. Straight stitch (see page 20) around each flower, using matching sewing thread.

4 Turn under 2cm along each edge of the strip and press. Then pin the strip 5cm from one side of the flannel, leaving a 2cm overlap at each end. Pin the overlaps to the back and sew the strip in place with short straight stitches around the edge, using matching sewing thread.

5 Decorate the towel in the same way.

LAUNDER THE APPLIQUÉ FABRIC, THE TOWEL AND FACE CLOTH AT THE MAXIMUM RECOMMENDED TEMPERATURE BEFORE YOU START WORK; NEW TOWELLING INEVITABLY SHRINKS WHEN FIRST WASHED.

Baby Towel

Cath Kidston

SKILL RATING: 2
WHAT YOU WILL NEED...

- White hooded baby towel
- Bondaweb
- Iron and pressing cloth
- Felt: 10 x 15cm pink; 10cm square
  each of red and light stone;
  scrap of dark brown
- Fleece: 10cm square of dark stone
- Plain cotton fabric: 10cm square
  of green
- Sewing thread to match fabrics
- Embroidery thread in dark brown
- Sewing workbox (see page 15)

This hooded baby towel, decorated with the charming songbird motif, makes a useful and pretty gift to welcome a new arrival.

1 You will find the reversed outline of this motif on the Songbird template card. Increase the size by 275% so that it fits inside the hood.

2 Following the dotted line, trace the underbody onto Bondaweb, then draw the other parts of the bird. Cut out roughly, and then fuse them onto felt: the body to light stone felt, the 'cheek' to pink, the breast to red, the beak and foot to dark brown. Always use a pressing cloth when ironing felt.

3 On a cool setting, iron the wing and tail to the back of the fleece. Cut all the shapes out carefully and peel off the backings.

4 Using the pressing cloth, iron the bird's body to the centre of the hood. Layer the other parts on top, then fuse the beak and foot to the towel. Work a few straight stitches for the eye (see page 20), using dark brown embroidery thread.

5 Complete the design with the two roses. Trace all the remaining elements onto Bondaweb, then cut the flowers from pink, red, light stone and brown felt, and the leaves and stems from green cotton. Remove the papers.

6 Position the roses on either side of the bird, then add the flower centres and the petals. Tuck the stems and leaves under the edges and iron in place, again using the pressing cloth.

7 Secure each appliqué piece to the background with a round of tiny straight stitches, using matching sewing thread.

TO PROTECT THE APPLIQUÉ, HAND WASH THE TOWEL IN COLD WATER ONLY WHEN NECESSARY, AND TRY TO AVOID GETTING THE HOOD WET.

Starry Fleece Blanket

Cath Kidston

SKILL RATING: 3
WHAT YOU WILL NEED...

- Pink fleece blanket
- Fleece: 60cm x 1m red
- Tacking thread
- Sewing thread in red
- Sewing workbox (see page 15)

Teddies and toddlers alike will want to cosy up under this warm, lightweight blanket.

1 The outline motifs for this project are on the Stars template card. To make the paper patterns, pick out four or five different stars and enlarge them by 200%. Cut out the photocopied stars around the outline.

2 Pin the patterns to the right side of the fleece and cut them out. My blanket measured 60cm by 100cm and is covered with 45 evenly spaced stars – you will need to make more for a larger blanket or fewer for a smaller one.

3 Arrange the stars across the blanket, balancing the arrangement of size and shape. Pin them in place when you are pleased with the composition, then tack down close to the edge.

4 Sew the stars to the blanket by working a round of straight stitches around the outside edge of each one (see page 20), using matching red sewing thread.

FLEECE FABRIC SHOULD NOT BE IRONED, SO A TRADITIONAL
METHOD OF HAND-STITCHED APPLIQUÉ IS USED HERE TO
SECURE THE STARS TO THE FLUFFY BLANKET.

Rose
Gloves

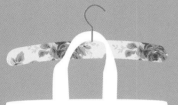

Cath Kidston

SKILL RATING: 3
WHAT YOU WILL NEED...

- Pair of cashmere gloves
- Lightweight non-woven iron-on interfacing
- Dressmaker's fading-ink pen
- Iron and pressing cloth
- Embroidery thread in pink, red, antique white, dark brown and green
- Sewing workbox (see page 15)

Keep your fingers toasty warm on the coldest day with these embroidered gloves. The rose detail makes them completely unique.

1 Photocopy the single rose outline on the right of the Songbird template card at 115%, then make a second, reversed enlargement. Lay a piece of interfacing over the first motif with the smooth (non-adhesive) side upwards. Using a fading pen, draw over the lines.

2 Trim the motif around the outside edge. Fuse the iron-on interfacing to the centre of the cuff with a cool iron and a pressing cloth.

3 Fill in each area with satin stitch (see page 20). Start with the pink petals, then the red and antique white. Finish the rose with a dark brown centre. Work the leaves in green, slanting the stitches on each side towards the centre.

4 Embroider the other rose onto the second glove in the same way, so that you have a matching pair.

IF YOU ENJOY STITCHING ON KNITWEAR, YOU COULD MAKE A COMPLETE WINTER ACCESSORY SET. WORK A SINGLE MOTIF ON EACH GARMENT OR SCATTER SEVERAL ACROSS A BERET OR ALONG A MATCHING SCARF.

Be
Inspired

It was very difficult to decide which projects to include in the book, as each design would work equally well on so many different items. Whether it's the sailing-boat on a T-shirt, cushion or bag, or the strawberries along the edge of a bed sheet, tea towel or skirt, the variations are endless. Over the next few pages I have laid out some further ideas for you, but half the fun will be choosing for yourself what to customise and how, using the techniques you have learnt.

Be Inspired

T-shirt

T-shirts are one of the cheapest and easiest items to adapt. Why not initial t-shirts and give them away as personalised gifts? Remember, you don't only have to work on the front; think about decorating the sleeves and the back of the t-shirt as well.

Beret

If you liked the beret on page 90, you could customise a woolly hat in the same way – great for a ski holiday! You could also embroider a simple design onto the hat – perhaps one of the rose motifs to give a prettier, more delicate look to the beret.

Skirt

Plain appliqué would work well on a patterned skirt, as it will contrast with the background design. Or you could layer up other prints for a great 'patchwork' effect. You could just decorate around the hem if the whole skirt is a bit daunting.

Tote Bag

You can pick up cheap eco bags all over the place and they are ideal for working on as they are such a simple shape. Consider embroidering over simple appliqué designs to create a textured, layered effect. You could also add a handy pocket inside, as shown on the strawberry apron (page 32). So that the stitching isn't visible on the outside, first make a simple lining and attach the pocket to that.

Apron

You could add one larger pocket to your apron using the same technique outlined on page 32. The breakfast template would work well here – maybe a row of boiled eggs or cups and saucers along the bottom? Or for a simpler project, why not cover the whole apron in colourful spots?

Jumper

There's now no need to throw out a much-loved, but tired old jumper. You can easily disguise moth holes and worn elbows using scraps of patterned fabric. Or you could embroider a simple motif onto the front in place of the initials on page 80.

Be Inspired

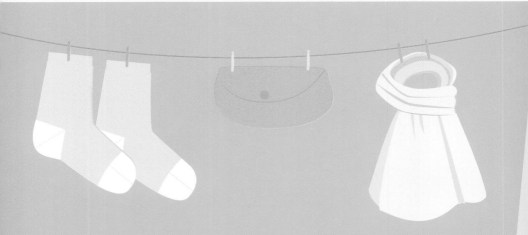

Socks

As well as embroidering onto bed socks, what about thick walking socks or giving a pair of personalised baby bootees as a gift? The embroidery method used on page 50 would also work well added to a jumper as a single motif.

Purse

Why not decorate a purse and use it as 'wrapping' for a precious present like a piece of jewellery? You could cover the whole purse in embroidery, or keep it simple with a single design on the back. Maybe you could match your purse to one of the designs in the bags chapter, or make either a shawl or scarf using the same template?

Scarf

If you liked our racing car scarf on page 86, why not try another design? You could appliqué spots or flowers all the way up it? Or you could spell out your favourite team name to make your own football scarf! Jersey fabric is cheap to buy and doesn't fray – a fantastic way to make yourself an instant scarf!

Oven Glove and Pot Holder

Why not take the colours of your own home as the palette for your kitchen accessories to make a really chic look. You could make some matching tea towels (as shown on page 26) and an apron (page 32). Any of the templates would work with these items – maybe you could have a very simple spotty theme running throughout the kitchen?

Tea Cosy

You can easily make a tea cosy by cutting up an old blanket and blanket-stitching around the curved edges. You could use the cup and saucer template to great effect here. If you're feeling ambitious, the country cottage would be a more traditional design to use (see page 56).

Picture Frame

A dusty old frame can quickly be transformed with a lick of gloss paint. Think about making a set of pictures by using different sections of the same template, or the same template completed in contrasting colours.

Addresses

Haberdasheries and fabric shops

A1 Fabrics
50–2 Goldhawk Road
London, W12 8DH
020 8740 7349

Abakhan Fabrics
34–44 Stafford Street
Liverpool, L3 8LX
0151 207 4029
www.abakhan.co.uk

C & H Fabrics
2 St. George's Street
Canterbury
Kent, T1 2SR
01227 459760
www.candh.co.uk

Edinburgh Fabrics
12–4 St. Patrick Square
Edinburgh, EH8 9EZ
0131 668 2790

John Lewis
Oxford Street
London, W1A 1EX
www.johnlewis.com

Liberty
Regent Street
London, W1B 5AH
020 7734 1234
www.liberty.co.uk

Textile King
81 Berwick Street
London, W1F 8TW
020 7437 7372

Truro Fabrics
Lemon Quay
Truro
Cornwall, TR1 2LW
01872 222130
www.shop.trurofabrics.com

Arts and Crafts

Audacious
Blackfriars
Monk Street
Newcastle upon Tyne, NE1 4XN
0191 232 6177

Craft Wise
5 Merrion Way
Merrion Centre
Leeds, LS2 8DB
0113 293 0636
www.craft-fair.co.uk/craftwise

CreativeMatters
7a Bridge Street
Bath, BA2 4AS
01225 446 996

London Graphic Centre
16–8 Shelton Street
London, WC2H 9JL
020 7759 4500
www.londongraphics.co.uk

The Guild of London Craftsmen
Jubilee Hall
The Piazza
London, WC2E 8BE
020 7240 5404

Vintage Clothing

Absolute Vintage
15 Hanbury Street
London, E1
020 7247 3883
www.absolutevintage.co.uk

Close to Spitalfields market, best for accessories, shoes and boots for men and women.

Armstrongs
81–3 Grassmarket
Edinburgh , EH1 2HJ
0131 220 5557
www.armstrongsvintage.co.uk

Great for traditional Scottish
highland wear and fabrics such
as tweed and cashmere.

Clifton Hill Antique Textiles
4–5 Lower Clifton Hill
Bristol, BS8 1BT
0117 929 0644

Clothes accessories and textiles
from Georgian
to modern.

Cloud Cuckoo Land
6 Charlton Place
Camden Passage
Islington, N1 8AJ
0207 354 3141

Pretty silk nighties, cashmere
cardigans and a good selection
of accessories.

Clobber
920 Christchurch Road
Bournemouth
Dorset
01202 433 330
www.vintageclobber.com

Particularly good for 1950s' and
1960s' clothing.

eBay
www.ebay.co.uk.

A great place to find vintage
clothes and collectables.

Past Caring
6 Chapel Yard
Albert Street
Holt
Norfolk, NR25 6HG
01263 713 771
www.4trewince.co.uk

A lovely little shop which carries
a huge amount of linen sheets,
pillow cases, curtains and
doilies.

Starry Starry Night
19 Dowanside Lane
Glasgow, D12 9BZ

Fantastic for bargain lace,
ribbons, tweeds and satins.
Popular with students.

The Vintage Clothing Company
Affleck's Palace
52 Church Street
Manchester, M1 1PW
0161 832 0548
www.afflecks.com

Every stall sells something
unique.

Urban Village
The Custard Factory
Gibb Street
Birmingham, B9 4AA
0121 244 5160
www.urban-village.co.uk

Masses of 1950s' to 1980s'
goods.

Markets

Bermondsey Market
Long Lane and Bermondsey
Street
London, SE1

Camden Market
Camden High Street
London , NW1

Portobello Market
Portobello Road
Ladbroke Grove End
London, W10 and W11

Snoopers Paradise
7–8 Kensington Gardens
Brighton
Sussex, BN1 4AL

**Vintage Fashion, Textiles
and Accessories Fair**
Hammersmith Town Hall
King Street
London, W6 9JU

Antiques Fairs

Ardingly International Antiques and Collectors Fair
South of England Showground
Ardingly
West Sussex
www.dmgantiquefairs.com

Newark International Antique and Collectors Fair
Newark and Nottinghamshire
Showground
Newark-on-Trent
Nottinghamshire
www.dmgantiquefairs.com

Shepton Mallet Antique Fair
Royal Bath and West
Showground
Shepton Mallet
Somerset, BA4 6QN
www.bathandwest.com

Sunbury Antiques Market
Kempton Park Racecourse
Sunbury-on-Thames
Middlesex, TW16 5AQ
01932 782292

A few handy websites:

www.barnyarns.co.uk
www.buttoncompany.co.uk
www.cottoncanvastotebags
.co.uk
www.craftynotions.com
www.josyrose.com
www.pennylaneuk.com
www.rustyzipper.com
www.sewessential.co.uk
www.soulrevolver.com

Cath Kidston's shops

Bath
3 Broad Street
Milsom Place
Bath, BA1 5LJ
01225 331 006

Battersea
142 Northcote Road
Battersea
London, SW11 6RD
020 7228 6571

Brighton
31a & 32 East Street
Brighton, BN1 1HL
01273 227 420

Bristol
79 Park Street
Clifton
Bristol, BS1 5PF
0117 930 4722

Chelsea
12 Cale Street
London, SW3 3QU
020 7584 3232

Cheltenham
21 The Promenade
Cheltenham, GL50 1LE
01242 245 912

Chiswick
125 Chiswick High Road
London, W4 2ED
020 8995 8052

Covent Garden
28–32 Shelton Street
London, WC2H 9JE
020 7836 4803

Dublin
Unit CSD 1.3
Dundrum Shopping Centre
Dublin 14

Edinburgh
58 George Street
Edinburgh, EH2 2LR
0131 220 1509

Fulham
668 Fulham Road
London, SW6 5RX
020 7731 6531

Guildford
14–18 Chertsey Street
Guildford, GU1 4HD
01483 573201

Harrogate
4–6 James Street
Harrogate, HG1 1RF
01423 531481

Holland Park
8 Clarendon Cross
London, W11 4AP
020 7221 4000

Kildare
Unit 21c Kildare Village
Nurney Road
Kildare Town
00 353 45 535 084

Kings Road
322 Kings Road
London
SW3 5UH
020 7351 7335

Kingston
10 Thames Street,
Kingston upon Thames
KT1 1PE
020 8546 6760

Liverpool
18 School Lane
Liverpool
L1 3BT
0151 709 2747

Marylebone
51 Marylebone High Street
London
W1U 5HW
020 7935 6555

Notting Hill
158 Portobello Road
London
W11 2BE

St Ives
67 Fore Street
St Ives
TR26 1HE
01736 798001

Tunbridge Wells
59–61 High Street
Tunbridge Wells
TN1 1XU
01892 521197

Wimbledon Village
3 High Street
Wimbledon
SW19 5DX
020 8944 1001

Winchester
46 High Street
Winchester
SO23 9BT
01962 870620

York
23 Stonegate
York
YO1 8AS
01904 733653

Concessions in:
Harvey Nichols, Knightsbridge, London
Selfridges, The Bull Ring, Birmingham
Selfridges, Oxford Street, London
Selfridges, Trafford Centre, Manchester
Bicester Village (outlet store), Oxfordshire

Acknowledgements

Many thanks to Jess Pemberton for making all of the projects, Pia Tryde, Karina Mamrowicz, Jenny Walker, Laura Mackay, Jo Sanders, Bridget Bodoano, Elaine Ashton and Lucinda Ganderton. Thanks also to Katherine Case, Laura Herring, Anne Furniss and Helen Lewis at Quadrille. This book is dedicated to Stanley.

Editorial Director: Anne Furniss
Art Director: Helen Lewis
Project Editor: Laura Herring
Designer: Katherine Case
Photographer: Pia Tryde
Illustrations: Bridget Bodoano, Laura Mackay
Project Designer and Maker: Jessica Pemberton
Needlework Consultant: Lucinda Ganderton
Pattern Checker: Sally Harding
Production Director: Vincent Smith
Production Controller: Ruth Deary

This edition published in 2010 by Quadrille Publishing Limited
Alhambra House
27–31 Charing Cross Road
London WC2H oLS
First published in 2008

Text copyright © Cath Kidston 2008
Design templates and projects © Cath Kidston 2008
Photography © Pia Tryde 2008
Design and layout copyright © Quadrille Publishing Limited 2008

Cataloguing-in-Publication Data: a catalogue record for this book is available from the British Library.

ISBN 978 184400 825 4

Printed in China

Templates

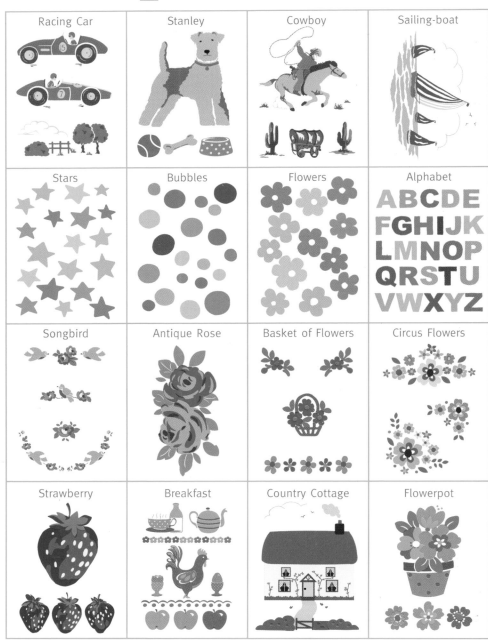

Racing Car	Stanley	Cowboy	Sailing-boat
Stars	Bubbles	Flowers	Alphabet
Songbird	Antique Rose	Basket of Flowers	Circus Flowers
Strawberry	Breakfast	Country Cottage	Flowerpot

ABCDE
FGHIJK
LMNOP
QRSTU
VWXYZ